A Chronology of
Men, Matters and Events

On My 90th Birthday

On the scale of today I contemplate
That I was born nine decades past,
In the march of time on the stage,
When others saw me perform the roles I played,
That have shaped me to be what I am today.

On my start, I learnt and fought,
And I began to walk on my chosen path
It led me to see the level what I thought
To be my base of higher goals that I sought
In the struggle that has no naught.

I have to fight the negative factors of my life
To score higher and survive
Hours full of days and nights
To become yearnings in the balance of my fated life.

Who am I? Do I not have the same colour and face?
Am I not from the same creed and race?
What meaning and measure do I seek as I advance in age?

Have I passed or failed, I cannot say,
I stand alone on the side of the roaring sea
To slip along to the final resting place of eternity.

Dharam Vir Taneja

A Chronology of Men, Matters and Events

Dharam Vir Taneja

HAR-ANAND
PUBLICATIONS PVT LTD

HAR-ANAND PUBLICATIONS PVT LTD
E-49/3, Okhla Industrial Area, Phase-II, New Delhi-110020
Tel.: 41603490
E-mail: info@haranandbooks.com/haranand@rediffmail.com
Shop online at: www.haranandbooks.com

Copyright © Dharam Vir Taneja, 2014

Reprint, 2018

All rights reserved. No part of this publication may be reproduced, stored in a retrieval system, or transmitted in any form or by any means, electronic, mechanical photocopying, recording or otherwise, without the prior written permission of the publishers.

Published by Ashok Gosain and Ashish Gosain for
Har-Anand Publications Pvt Ltd

Printed in India

Acknowledgements

The urge to write a book concerning my life occurred to me in my mid-80s. I will attain the age of 90 years on the 4th of July 2014. I have reached a stage in my life when I need to refresh my memory and recall the minutiae of events in my life concerning the various personalities I encountered during my professional career as a banker and as an economist. The impact of these events and personalities prompted me to pen my thoughts and recollections in this book. I enjoy writing and this book gave me the opportunity to present these thoughts and recollections in an organized manner.

I am being looked after under the overall care and concern of my wife, Kamal, to whom I owe a great debt of gratitude. I sought the help of my elder daughter Rashmi to review the manuscript. With her mastery of the English language (Rashmi holds a Master's Degree in English Literature from the University of London), I was assured that my work was meticulously vetted by her. I am very grateful to her for her constant care and devotion.

In order to give a final touch to the manuscript, I turned to my younger daughter, Ramni, and asked her whether she could accommodate me and help me despite her busy professional life as a practising Advocate in various courts in

Delhi and India, including the Supreme Court of India. She readily agreed to help me and as a consequence of her caring support, I have been able to complete this book. During the last six months, Ramni has spent a considerable amount of time reviewing the manuscript, discussing its content with me and finally presenting these pages that grace themselves in this work. Her contribution has been most valuable and timely.

I owe my thanks to everyone in my family, i.e. Kamal, Rashmi and Ramni who, through mutual coordination, ensured that *A Chronology of Men, Matters and Events* saw the light of day.

I also wish to thank Sanjeev Kumar Jha, who helped me during the last few years to type my handwritten manuscript.

I am extremely grateful to Mr Narendra Kumar, Chairman, Har-Anand Publications Pvt Ltd, New Delhi for his kindness, support and his gracious patience in publishing this book. It is through the kind courtesy of Mr Kumar that this book will reach its readers.

I dedicate this book to the emerging new India.

Dharam Vir Taneja

Preface

In 2006, it dawned on me that true pictures of my life, starting from childhood, jolted my mind and left an indelible impression on my memory. Hence, I felt an urge to write them down. The process of delving into my past has continued unabated and these events having been recorded by way of handwritten notes have eventually been crystallized into this book, entitled *A Chronology of Men, Matters and Events*.

Naturally, most of the anecdotes which have made their place in this piece of work have now become an intrinsic part of my life. Whether these relate to my grandparents or to eminent people decorating the annals of our time, I applied a test that I would record only those stories where I was personally involved and those persons or personalities who have touched my life. What is narrated here concerns events, occurrences, incidents, affairs, matters, episodes, averments, facts, and phenomena that occurred, that were a part of my life and that eventually became an integral part of my being.

As I shifted my attention from one true event to another, wherever discretion was required, I consciously omitted a few events that were strictly confidential. I request my readers to bear with me on this ground.

Most of my life has been spent in a continuous struggle, which raged in my mind. This intense debate in the innermost recesses of my mind was a witness to a battle between me and my inner self.

Dharam Vir Taneja

Contents

I	Introduction	11
II	My Grandmother's Charkha Club Funeral of Bhagat Singh and His Associates	18
III	The Arya Samaj and the Gurukul	21
IV	Lahore	24
V	The Early Days and My Sense of Justice	29
VI	More Injuries and Illnesses	40
VII	Life in Lahore: 1935-1940	42
VIII	Lahore High Court	46
IX	D.A.V. College, Lahore: 1940-1944	48
X	Dawn of Corruption and Debate on Partition	51
XI	Career with PNB, Lahore and Partition and Independence of India	58
XII	Run on the Punjab National Bank Ltd (1949)	65
XIII	Mahatma Hansraj and My Association with Lala Yodhraj	75
XIV	The Punjab National Bank Ltd: Dalmia-Jain Group	83
XV	New Innings at the Central Bank of India and Meeting Pandit Nehru	94
XVI	A Stint with Literature: 1946 Onwards and India's Leaders Post-Independence	102

XVII	My Association with Central Bank of India	113
XVIII	Report of the Commission of Enquiry on Maruti Affairs	139
XIX	Vignettes of Some Leading Bankers of Central Bank of India	155
XX	Nani Palkhivala: The TCS Story	161
XXI	Eminent Personalities in Independent India	169
XXII	Interactions with Mrs Indira Gandhi	185
XXIII	The Middle East: Dubai and the United Arab Emirates	195
XXIV	Reserve Bank of India	205
XXV	Thoughts on Black Money	211
XXVI	Postscript: The Silence of the Unknown	222

1
Introduction

The novelist creates artificial characters.

In this book, entitled *A Chronology of Men, Matters and Events,* I, the author,[1] having been an Indian and international banker, an economist and a poet, and nearing the age of 90 on 4.7.2014, have (in contrast to the proverbial novelist), woven around myself approximately 100 true stories that occurred in my life from childhood to my working life up to the age of 77, covering an uninterrupted span of over seven decades. I was born on 4 July 1924, in Quetta, Baluchistan, in what was then undivided India. I have lived in India, UK and the UAE and my career as a banker has spanned different parts of the world and, of course, India. This book chronicles seven decades of history, banking and economics, both in India and overseas, from the perspective of a national and international banker, who is also, incidentally, a poet. I have endeavoured, to the best of my ability, to narrate interesting events, peppered with true anecdotes and reminiscences of my role in Indian as well as international banking. I have presented to the reader, a

---

[1] Former Chairman and Managing Director of Central Bank of India and former Chief General Manager and Vice Chairman of the Executive Committee, Middle East Bank Ltd., Dubai, United Arab Emirates.

veritable journey of true and courageous stories. I have witnessed and experienced the painful and tragic partition of India leading to the creation of Pakistan. As the story of my life unfolds through the course of this book, I explain how I rose from a very humble position as a junior clerk to the highest position as Chairman and Managing Director of a nationalized bank in 1974-1975. I subsequently headed an international bank in the Middle East i.e. Dubai between 1984 and 1989.

In this book, I have also recalled from my memory true stories concerning my parents, grandparents, school and college days, a debate in the Government College Lahore on the partition of the country, and the personality and role of Mahatma Hans Raj in the DAV movement. I have extensively explained my role in the Punjab National Bank Limited (PNB), where I started my career in 1944 as a junior clerk, initially in Lahore, in undivided India, to New Delhi, India. In 1956, I moved to the Central Bank of India Ltd. (CB) after working as a Public Relations Officer and economic advisor in PNB. By this time, the Dalmia Jain Group controlled PNB. This book explains my encounters with Seth Shanti Prasad Jain, who was then the Chairman of PNB, and due to a clash of views and perspectives with him, I was compelled to quit PNB.

This book also refers to events in 1963 when I released my book of 51 poems, spanning over 180 pages, entitled, *Reflections in a Mirror,* in New Delhi, dedicated to Pandit Jawaharlal Nehru, whom I described in my book of poems as a 'treasured jewel among men'. Pandit Nehru accepted this dedication on 21 September 1963. Earlier, in 1961, I had taken the same manuscript to Dr. S. Radhakrishnan, who was at that time the Vice-President of India, and had requested him to write a Foreword to my book of poems. Dr. Radhakrishnan later wrote to me in his letter dated 6 July 1961: *Your enthusiasm and linguistic equipment are impressive. I do not think the book requires any foreword.* This book of poems has now been re-published in the USA.

In the present book, there are recollections concerning my interaction with the Government of India and the then Prime Minister of India, Mrs. Indira Gandhi at the relevant time, i.e., between 1969 to 1970, when I was asked by P. N. Haksar, Principal Private Secretary to Prime Minister Indira Gandhi, to prepare notes on economic matters on the topics suggested by the Prime Minister. I recall that Mrs. Gandhi was so impressed by the quality of these notes and presentation that she asked me to join her team. I indicated that I would only do so if I could retain my lien on my job in the Central Bank of India. Mrs. Gandhi and I remained in touch after I was transferred from Bombay (present day Mumbai) to London in 1971 through one of her Cabinet colleagues, more specifically to get my views on a scheme how to deal with black money. During my posting in London (1971-1973), I headed the branch of Central Bank of India. Earlier, in May, 1970, I had been deputed in a series of assignments by the Government of India to assist the London branch of the Central Bank of India, in unearthing a fraud that took place between 1968-1970. The enormity of the fraud had shaken the Central Bank of India and it was also considered at the relevant time, one of the major international frauds in the United Kingdom.

Significantly, the book records certain key events in my career as a banker in India during the 1960s till 1975. In 1964, I was transferred from Delhi to Bombay, the headquarters of the Central Bank of India. The Government of India appointed me as Chairman and Managing Director of Central Bank of India in 1974. After the expiry of my term in 1975, the Governor, Reserve Bank of India and the then Finance Minister recommended an extension of four years for my term as Chairman and Managing Director. However, Mrs. Indira Gandhi, the Prime Minister at the time, overruled their recommendations and did not give me an extension, leading to the termination of my services. I became one of the first victims of the Emergency in the banking world in India at the relevant time, i.e., in 1975. In the report of the Commission of Inquiry on Maruti Affairs dated 31 May 1979, Justice A.C. Gupta (who was at the relevant time on the Bench of the Supreme Court of India), in his findings concerning the investigation into the affairs of Maruti Limited, concluded:[2] *From the facts, the conclusion seems inescapable that Prime Minister Shrimati Indira Gandhi opposed the renewal of Shri Taneja's term as Chairman of Central Bank of India overruling the recommendations of the Reserve Bank of India and the Finance Minister because Taneja did not find it possible to approve Sanjay Gandhi's proposal for a loan of Rs. 1.5 crores to help Maruti Limited.*

---

[2]Chapter VIII, p. 129.

The book further records the facts that in 1975, when there was turmoil all around in India and the debate in the Rajya Sabha was taking place on my removal as Chairman and Managing Director of the Central Bank of India, Nani Palkhivala, the celebrated and renowned jurist who was also Vice-Chairman of Tata Sons, the holding company, invited me to join the Tata Group, which I did on 1 January 1976 at Tata Chemicals Ltd. From 1 April 1976, I was additionally attached to Tata Consultancy Services as a consulting advisor, which I permanently joined from 1 January 1977. I enjoyed working with F.C. Kohli, who was then the Director in-charge of Tata Consultancy Services (TCS).

I left Tata Consultancy Services in May 1982, to take up an assignment with the Middle East Bank Ltd., Dubai, UAE. My decision saddened Mr. Kohli and two other Directors of the Tata Group. I recall in this book how Mr. Kohli had given me shelter at a time when I was troubled and harassed by the then Prime Minister, Mrs. Indira Gandhi and her son, Sanjay Gandhi. In May 1975, Mrs. Gandhi, as Prime Minister, personally got an FIR (No 9/75) registered against me. I also recall that Mrs. Gandhi imposed an Emergency on 26 June 1975. The enquiry by the Central Bureau of Investigation (CBI) that was initiated against me by Indira Gandhi was dropped in 1976 by the CBI, for want of evidence and the case was closed.

Additional recollections in the book include my two decades spent in Dubai, UAE. This book presents a rare and personal glimpse into the world of international banking in the Middle East, from the perspective of an Indian and international banker, who headed the Middle East Bank Limited. I narrate in this book that Middle East Bank Limited was promoted in 1975 by a well-known and respected group in Dubai, headed by Majid Al Futtaim. This bank had expanded at a rather fast pace. Between 1981 and 1982, the Bank was located in 12 other locations of the world, including five in Africa. In April 1984, I took over the management of the Bank as the Chief General Manager and Vice-Chairman of its Executive Committee. In February 1989, the Chairman of the Bank, Majid Al Futtaim asked me to resign and another group took over the management of the Middle East Bank Limited. The balance sheet of Middle East Bank Limited for the year 1990 was not approved by the Central Bank of the UAE. In 1991, the Government of Dubai took over Middle East Bank Limited. My professional services continued to be availed by Abdulla Al Futtaim, who was (with Majid Al Futtaim) fifty per cent co-owner in all enterprises of the Al Futtaim Group at the relevant time. His son, Omar Al Futtaim, floated Al Futtaim Sons LLC, which I joined in 1991. In 1997, I left Al Futtaim Sons but continued my association with Abdulla Al Futtaim and Omar Al Futtaim till I left for India in October 2001. In 2001, Abdulla Al Futtam took charge of the business enterprises of the Al Futtaim Group in Dubai and the UAE.

My association with His Highness, Sheikh Hasher bin Juma Al Maktoum, a member of the Ruling Family of Dubai, began in 1995 and continued till I returned to India in October 2001 at the age of 77.

In May 2002, I underwent a major heart surgery, i.e., a triple bypass. I now lead a retired and restful life. I keep myself busy in finalizing a manuscript of my proposed new book: *Economics of India*. I also propose to release another volume of my book of new poems.

POST SCRIPTUM: SILENCE OF THE UNKNOWN

In December 1978, I felt that my mind gave up its active mode and transferred itself to the mode of the silence of the unknown. Ever since then, I have continued to treasure and experience this silence. I have been recording notes on what this silence means. These notes will form the subject matter of a book when published. This future book will also record the intense intellectual mental struggle I have experienced over a span of 20 years between 1958 to 1978. Eventually, I arrived at the conclusion that the foundation of peace of mind lies in love and truth.

2
My Grandmother's Charkha Club Funeral of Bhagat Singh and His Associates

Gandhiji's stature as a crusader, leading the war against the British, and his hold over the masses in the struggle for India's independence, held the people electrified and morally uplifted, based on his principles of *satyagraha,* truth and non-violence. He created the cult of the spinning wheel, i.e., the *charkha* as a symbol for identification with the poorest of the country who did not have enough to cover their bodies.

My grandmother, Dhan Devi (1876-1957), who was greatly influenced by Gandhiji, took to spinning and the cult of the *charkha.* She along with a few other ladies in the neighbourhood formed a club, called the *Charkha Club,* which held its meetings in different houses where they performed mass spinning and sang patriotic songs in tune with the humming sound of the spinning wheel. I often accompanied her to these meetings.

An event that left an indelible impression on my mind was the funeral procession of Bhagat Singh, Sukhdev and Rajguru. In 1929, the three freedom fighters had thrown a bomb in the Legislative Assembly in New Delhi. They had been sentenced to death by hanging, following a sham trial for their involvement in the Lahore Conspiracy Case.

Since the three revolutionaries were from the Punjab and had taken the extreme step of waging war against the British, they had become national heroes. They had emotionally unified the country with their daring acts of heroism. In the prevailing surcharged atmosphere, my grandmother, choking with barely suppressed anger, announced she would carry me on her shoulders to join the funeral procession on 24 March 1931, to watch the cremation of these three heroes.

I was barely seven then. It appears that the pleas of my grandfather and my parents that the route of the procession was very long, and, that the cremation would take place at some distance on the banks of the river Ravi, and that I should be spared this ordeal, went unheeded by my grandmother. I was too small to endure this long journey, they pleaded. I would be hungry and thirsty, they pleaded again.

My grandmother, who was by now heading a brigade of twenty other women in our neighbourhood, assured my grandfather that they would take enough water and food for me and bring me home safe at night.

There are two events of that day which I vividly remember. The procession had about 30,000 mourners (figures from subsequent accounts as published in a book on Bhagat Singh) including 5,000 women, all dressed in mourning clothes. At the first crossing, the women sat down on the road and began beating their chests in a long tormenting wail of a dirge, crying and shouting slogans against the British. People stood on their balconies showering flowers on us. I started crying profusely along with the ladies. I have no recollection of what happened thereafter, until the procession reached the banks of the river Ravi. I was totally exhausted and I discovered that I was now being carried on the shoulders of some other female mourner. My grandmother woke me up to see the flames rise in the sky. What followed were cries of anguish, the sobs of the mourners and more impassioned slogans denouncing the autocratic rule of the British.

3
The Arya Samaj and the Gurukul

The Arya Samaj was a very powerful movement in the Punjab. The Arya Samaj was founded by Swami Dayanand Saraswati (1824-1883) in 1875. It represented the progressive and reformist sections of society. Swami Dayanand did not believe in idol worship and other traditional rituals. He was a towering personality, a renowned and distinguished scholar in Sanskrit, and he gave a scientific interpretation to the *Vedas*. He propagated the belief in the one and invisible all-pervasive power. He advocated self-discipline, and promoted an idealistic, frugal, simple and disciplined life. He caught the imagination of the middle classes in North-Western India. His message continues to be carried forward through a band of followers, who were inspired by his spiritual and moral status. The Arya Samaj is a very powerful movement in the north-west of India.

The Dayanand Anglo Vedic or D.A.V. Movement (1886) started by Mahatma Hansraj (1864-1938) believed in education, social reform, emancipation of women, widow remarriage, and the complete abolition of the caste system. The movement also proposed that members of the lowest caste could also be trained to be priests. By 1911, the members of the Arya Samaj had risen to over 100,000.

Differences, however, surfaced among the followers of Swami Dayanand, the founder of Arya Samaj. Two factions emerged in 1892.

Lala Munshi Ram (later Swami Shradhanand) (1857-1926) represented the other faction. He strongly believed that food must be vegetarian and Sanskrit be given prime importance in the school syllabus. In 1903, he established Gurukul Kangri (Assembly of Teachers University in Sanskrit) at Kankhal, a village near Haridwar on the banks of the river Ganges.

My grandmother, Dhan Devi, was a woman of strong convictions. She had six surviving children. My grandmother insisted that my father, (1894 to 1986), the eldest and only son, be educated in Gurukul Kangri where he spent 14 years. He was given the name *Atmanand* by the Gurukul (his original name was Hemraj). He graduated from there in Botany and Chemistry in 1918. The main emphasis of his education was erudition in Sanskrit; the second language was Hindi, although the science subjects were taught in English.

The British recognized the D.A.V. College and approved its affiliation to the Punjab University, whose students were allowed to take examinations from matriculation onwards. Students graduating from the Gurukul were not entitled to take the competitive exams of the Punjab or any recognized university and, thus, were not entitled to join government service. They were also considered a potential threat to the British Raj.

After graduation and later throughout his working life, my father could only find jobs as a teacher. We were three brothers. My elder brother, Dev Dutt Taneja (1920-2007), started his own business in 1940. My younger brother, Satya Vrat Taneja (1928 to 2013), joined the Punjab National Bank Ltd. in 1946 and later moved to the Bank of India Ltd., in 1963, from where he retired in 1988.

My father began his working life in Gujarat in 1920. After graduating from Gurukul, he was invited by Seth Ambalal Sarabhai, who was a founder industrialist in the textile business. He lived in Ahmedabad in a huge estate called 'Shahi Bagh'. Ambalal felt that his family members lived in great luxury and were not familiar with the development of Hindu philosophy. He employed my father to teach Sanskrit and oversee the moral and religious education of his children. He had also provided accommodation to all the private tutors of his children in the same estate where he lived. This assignment, however, was contractual.

After his contract was over, another progressive Gujarati group, led by Karuna Shankar, persuaded my father to shift to Kosindra, a village near Baroda (Varodara) where he started teaching Sanskrit. Thereafter, in 1926, we moved to Multan, where my father was offered a job at Gurukul, a school-level institution.

4
Lahore

My grandfather, Lala Dayal Chand (1871-1971) migrated from Karachi to Lahore in 1894, where some years earlier, he had settled in Karachi, having moved from Dera Ghazi Khan, the home of our ancestors. He joined Bharat Insurance Company Limited in 1894 in Lahore and was due for retirement in 1931. He had persuaded Lala Harkishan Lal, the Chairman and Founder of Bharat Insurance Company Limited, that in lieu of his long service, my father should be appointed in Bharat Insurance Company Limited. After the consent of his employers, he asked my father to relocate to Lahore.

My father reached Lahore in the middle of 1930 and started living, as was the custom, in a joint family, as part of my grandfather's extended family.

My father could not be persuaded to join a commercial organization. He did not want his education of 14 years to be sacrificed to the confines of an office where business considerations would overwhelm other priorities of life. He was young and idealistic, full of zeal and enthusiasm to work for the cause of the Arya Samaj. He preferred a job as an inspector of Arya Samaj schools, spread across different parts of the Punjab.

Upon my arrival in Lahore, I was faced with the complexity of a linguistic problem. At home my father, Pandit Atmanand, and my mother, Lajwati, (1899-1986) could speak basic Gujarati. My parents also conversed with each other in the Multani dialect called Saraiki, which is now used extensively in South Punjab in Pakistan. It appears I combined Saraiki with Gujarati and developed my own *lingua franca*. My grandfather told my grandmother that while at home I could speak in my mother tongue, but I should also learn Punjabi.

In the undivided Punjab, Urdu was the recognized language, and therefore it was decided that I should be admitted into a school where the medium of instruction was Urdu. Accordingly, I was left in the care of a maulvi (teacher), who started imparting formal lessons in Urdu daily on a part-time basis at a tuition fee of Rs. 2 per month. In the meantime, my teacher and grandmother helped me to pick up Punjabi also.

Having acquired the skills of writing in the Urdu alphabet, I was then sent to Sanatan Dharam School in the neighbourhood where, as a consequence of the persuasion of my parents and due to my ability to read and write fluently, I was promoted to Class 2. I was already late in studies by two years. During the course of my education, I remember having skipped Class 3 and only read seriously in Class 4.

My First Interaction with the Commercial World

While at the Sanatan Dharam School (1930-34), I had become my grandmother's sole purchase agent and ran various errands for her. She seemed to suffer from some mysterious gastric problems. Near our house at Gwal Mandi was a doctor's dispensary. Dr Narsingh Das had prescribed her a carminative mixture, which I had to bring every alternative day. Occasionally, she would give me a commission of one paisa. Once assured that I could move about in the neighborhood, she gave me two additional responsibilities: to purchase milk for the family after the cows had been milked in my presence, and to procure the groceries whenever needed. She had introduced me to the shopkeepers from whom I would do the purchasing. I recall that milk cost 2 *annas* a seer then. And from the grocery shop I bought pulses, wheat, soap, pure ghee, and matchboxes. The other sundry items, comprising fruits and vegetables, were purchased from vendors near the *subzi mandi* (vegetable market). I paid for all my purchases in cash and would sometimes even haggle with the shopkeepers about the rates. I remember the cost of wheat was around Rs. 2 and 6-8 *annas* per maund (40 seers) and the price of pulses 3-6 *annas* a seer. Pure ghee cost approximately Rs. 1 per seer. (Later, during the duration of the Second World War (1939-45) when prices soared, I was at war with myself and the shopkeepers as to why they were raising prices). My grandfather became my court of appeal to explain to me the rationale of this phenomenon called inflation. He had passed through a similar phase during the First World War (1914-18), but I continued to pursue my questioning and mentally refused to accept the new dispensation, as it adversely affected our family budget.

Aunty Satya's Nursery School

When I reached Lahore in 1930, my youngest aunt, Satya, was waiting to be engaged and married. As it used to happen decades ago in the lives of middle class families in India, messages were flashed everywhere indicating the requirement of a bridegroom. Various proposals were received, which were assessed, negotiated or fell through for one reason or the other until the right match was found. Aunty Satya was passing through the same phase. At that time, the girl was kept informed by her parents as to what was happening regarding her marriage alliance. It was also felt necessary that in the interim, she would, if it were possible, be preoccupied in terms of some kind of work scenario.

Some distance away from our house, Aunty Satya had started a nursery school where children between the ages of approximately 4 and 5 years, mostly girls, were admitted. After some weeks of my arrival, a suggestion was mooted that I should start my schooling from Aunty Satya's school. When the prescribed uniform had been prepared, one day Aunty Satya took me to the school. There were a total of 20 children in the school. The school had proper chairs and desks where all the children were comfortably seated. I was given a seat next to a girl right at the end of the class. I had not seen so many little girls, all having a red ribbon in their hair.

Out of curiosity, I touched the red ribbon of the girl seated next to me. The girl thought I was going to hit her so she punched me with her fist. In retaliation, I did likewise but gently, whereupon she shrieked and started crying. This brought my teacher aunty to our desk. For a few minutes we both got into an argument as to who hit whom first. At this juncture, my aunty asked me to accompany her when she seated me next to a boy. The class continued peacefully. While other students had far advanced in their lessons, she managed to teach me only three letters of the English alphabet—A B C.

When we went home, my grandfather, Babaji told me that he had been to a maulvi saheb, who would from the next day start giving me tuitions in Urdu. I was very excited about it. I accompanied Babaji to a nearby shop where he helped me to buy an Urdu alphabet book, *quaida, takhti, galaichi,* slate, *salaiti* and duster to start my serious studies.

5
The Early Days and My Sense of Justice

The year was 1931, and it was the season for Shujabad mangoes in Lahore. These were mature mangoes, whose pulp could be sucked quite easily. My mother, Lajwati (then aged 32) mentioned to me that she, accompanied by my grandmother (then aged 55), had visited the fruit market and bought mangoes in the Shujabad mango auction. They were able to buy a basket of mangoes for Rs. 1. The basket of mangoes contained 60 pieces. By that time, I had learnt to count up to one hundred. The ladies jointly said that half the quantity could be sent to some friend's house. On my suggestion, it was agreed that the gift be sent to my Urdu teacher, Maulvi Saheb, who lived not far away from our house. When after lunch every one in the family (eight members in all) had consumed their respective share of mangoes, a discussion started on how many mangoes were to be delivered to Maulvi Saheb.

The family lunch used to take place at about 11 o'clock in the morning whereafter all elderly members went about doing their chores. Then male members took rest and the ladies washed clothes. It was decided that since these were hot summer months, when the sun came down, someone would go and deliver the basket of mangoes to Maulvi Saheb.

When I was playing about, a thought crossed my mind that while my father had told me that he charged Rs.16 per month as tuition fee, the Maulvi was being paid Rs. 2 only. This was grave injustice. More particularly, we were going to send only 8 *annas* worth of mangoes. I went to my mother and conveyed my thoughts but she did not respond. I further told her that I would go on hunger strike for this reason.

It was a routine in our home that 3 to 4 hours after lunch, we children used to be given a banana plus sweetened glass of milk, which was usually heated. When my mother offered me these at the usual time, I told her I was on hunger strike. After refusing to take my banana-milk combination, I rejoined the children of the locality playing in the street opposite our house. More time passed, whereafter I returned to the house and started crying profusely. When I felt exhausted, I stretched myself, regained some strength and resumed crying again. Up till this stage, no one came to check on me. It was a big house and everybody was taking rest in their respective rooms. So I shifted to another part of the house where I resumed my wails so that people would hear me.

My grandfather heard my cries and between my sobs and deep breaths, I told him why I was on hunger strike and why I wanted Maulvi Saheb to be given an adequate quantity of mangoes. On his assurance and my agreement, he went to the bazar and bought 15 more Shujabad mangoes for me. I broke my fast. Then came the question of who would carry the basket, as the basket was heavy with 45 mangoes. Since I was not able to lift it, my mother agreed to carry the basket and we went and delivered it to my teacher.

SUMMER OF 1932 – LAHORE
THE HORROR AND PAIN OF SMALL POX

An event of serious magnitude was to occur involving my grandmother, Dhan Devi, then about 56 years old. It so happened that our entire family, my grandparents, two aunts, I and my father and my two brothers, were present on the occasion of the marriage of Vidya, daughter of Lala Niranjan Das. It was the evening of 1932. I was about 8 years old. Almost the entire Derawal community was in attendance. My father, who happened to touch me, was shocked to note that I was burning with high fever. My mother had been left at home to nurse my newborn sister. My father knew a doctor who was present among the many guests. He took me to meet him. The doctor examined me and told my father that as my temperature could be higher than 104, I should be carried back home and ice packs should be applied on my head to bring down the temperature. I must have overheard this conversation. My grandmother, whom we called 'Ammaji', offered to take me back as she knew my mother could not look after me along with my newborn sister.

At home, Ammaji started applying ice packs when after a while I went to sleep. I got up the next day. Ammaji told me that my fever had risen to 106 degrees in the previous evening but the ice packs helped to bring it down to 103^0. If ice packs were stopped, the temperature tended to rise again.

This condition continued in the next 4-5 days during which I stopped taking any solid food; instead, I asked for my homemade sweet drink laced with squeezed lemons.

On the fifth day, some eruptions started appearing on my body. They pained on being touched. At this stage Ammaji shifted me from a room in the second floor of the house to a partly covered terrace on the third floor. It had a toilet and a separate bathroom facility. She informed the other family members that the eruptions spreading all over my body were signs of the highly virulent small pox disease. Hence, I was to be kept in isolation on the terrace. No other family member was allowed to enter this isolated area. Food could be sent up through the facility of a rope, which could pull a tray from the lower floors.

At this stage I had no fever. The fast spread of boils in the body continued unabated. Ammaji told me that this type of small pox was known to take 40 days to heal.

She ordered large quantities of dry *neem* leaves. There was no part of my body where the boils had not spread. Even my hands—the front and back fingers—had painful eruptions. Since I could not eat with my hands, Ammaji started feeding me.

These were summer days when the heat is very intense in Lahore. Ammaji had a hand-held fan to keep the flies away. At night, I used to be shifted to the open terrace and during the day, I was moved to a partly covered area called *Barsati* (a place covered against rain). I could not stand as the soles of my feet and toes were covered with boils. Amma ji used to carry me as and when required. I was just an 8-year-old boy and in the second standard in school.

I started losing weight very fast. My chest disclosed all the bones that lay beneath and my face had shrunk as if I was a very sick child.

This was my condition on the 12th day when a white fluid started filling in all the eruptions, leading to more pain and greater discomfort all around.

I made a mental calculation and told Ammaji that 28 days had still to go, which meant almost a month before I would recover.

Ammaji used to tell me episodes from the *Ramayana* and *Mahabharata*. She also knew some stories like Hira-Panna, which she narrated to me to keep me entertained. She also used to sing patriotic songs. She told me who Gandhiji was and where he was at that time, when she last had news of him, since now she was cut off from her friends and didn't have the latest news on Gandhiji.

I could not any longer lie on the stringed bed as the pain was too intense and I would often cry. Ammaji lifted me and gave me the comfort of her lap where I used to be lying most of the time.

As I advanced in my illness, I was getting into the shape of a skeleton; it appeared as if the internal lining of my intestines had boils. I had to be shifted to liquid foods. When Ammaji was not telling me stories or not in conversations with me about the life of my father and how he was a great scholar of Sanskrit and knew all the *Vedas,* I used to be asleep.

Earlier on or about the seventh or eighth day, a day when I could not wear any clothes, Ammaji had spread neem leaves on my naked body. I used to lie on neem leaves and was also covered with neem leaves.

Half way through my illness, the disease of small pox was at its peak. All the eruptions had fully covered my face and the entire head. I could not bear the intensity of my illness and started pestering Ammaji with questions asking about my recovery.

Throughout the major part of my illness, I was fully covered with boils filled with while fluid, on my front and back of the body. Though I had no clothes but the proximity of eruptions on my naked body appeared to fill the purpose of clothes.

As Ammaji had predicted, with time the boils started shrinking and reducing in size. The white fluid began to disappear. However, a new brown thing appeared replacing the white-filled boils and slowly the brown replacement took the form of a dry leaf. This development was slow in appearance but the earlier discarding white substance had covered most of my body. Wherever any white eruption had emerged in my body, the same size brown permanent marks replaced it. I looked a new person with brown marks everywhere. At this stage, Ammaji decided to bathe me in pure ghee.

On the appointed day, which was the 42nd day, pure ghee was thoroughly rubbed on every part of my body. The process of rubbing was done repeatedly. After some time, I was given a bath of warm water. My clothes and the stringed bed on which I used to sleep were burnt under medical advice. I was to wear new clothes.

My father had made elaborate arrangements for a *Havan* ceremony where I was garlanded. My father said it was a welcome homecoming as if I were reborn. My grandparents, my parents and my aunts hugged me. They told me that they had lost all the hope that I would ever recover and survive this ordeal.

My father and mother individually thanked Ammaji, for having taken so good care of me and for saving me from the clutches of death when all the six children in the adjacent houses, with whom I used to play, perished as a consequence of the attack of the 40 days' long small pox.

I was in no position to resume my studies in school. I was in Class II. One of my aunts was given the responsibility to coach me Arithmetic. My mother would coach me Urdu text and the basic elements of grammar. My mother was educated in a government girls school in Sibi, where she lived before marriage. The medium of instruction this school was Urdu. She also went to Gurudwara private school in Sibi where the medium of instruction was Gurmukhi. She on her own efforts learn Hindi. Her family had briefed her well about Swami Dayanand and Arya Samaj. The Headmaster was kind enough, and he promoted me to Class III on humanitarian grounds. I was exempted from clearing my exams for Class II.

I was welcomed in Class III when the session started next year. Ammaji was my best friend. She looked after my recovery in the coming 6 months. She made me stand on my feet again and fed me with her own hands to ensure that I got the correct food supplement. My mother was occupied during this period with her newborn daughter.

Ammaji's concern for my welfare did not wane as time kept its march. I used to undress before her every week where she would count the deep brown marks which occupied my body like a beehive. They had started to lose their colour and merged with the light complexion of my skin. It was a slow process and I could report to her the developments on the front part of the body. She used to tell me about the progress concerning my head and back. By 1933, one year after the attack of small pox, the extremities, my hands and arms as well as my feet and legs, no longer had the numerous deep-seated brown marks. In other parts by the end of 1934, the depth of the colour was also losing its shade. In 1935, when I shifted my school, one could count the brown marks on one's fingers.

Ammaji took care of my scholastic progress very closely. I did not appear for Class III final examination as I was good in my studies. The only time I seriously studied was in the fourth standard in 1934, when I was ten years old. I was required to clear the final examination comprising a syllabus of six subjects.

After shifting my school in 1935, Ammaji took charge of me as a parent to ensure that I attended my studies and did my homework. She encouraged me to join the Boy Scout Movement as I had to regularly drill there. From the fifth standard onwards, I had another supervisor, Babaji, my grandfather. After school, I would narrate to him the day's events, particularly whatever happened on the road of four miles distance each way, to and from school, and about my teachers and the new friends I had made.

Ammaji persuaded me to join the hockey team in school. I only gained some height when I was 18 years old; until then, I remained short in stature and an easy victim of being hit in different parts of my legs whether I was playing hockey in offensive or defensive roles. The signs of these wounds are still visible on both my legs. I used to bleed profusely from my ankles and had bruises on different parts of the body. Playing hockey was serving no purpose so I was shifted to the cricket team where I continued playing until the end of the school term. The school used to supply kits, balls and bats. The municipality permitted us to play on their extended grounds.

Our grandparents had more than a score of grandchildren from their three daughters and a son. I had one elder brother and a younger brother. My sister sadly passed away in 1945. There was no occasion when my grandparents would not be making it a point to mention how much they were proud of me.

My grandmother died in Delhi at the age of 81 in 1957 due to cardiac failure. My grandfather passed away in Delhi in 1971, one month short of the age of 100 due to a fall when he hurt his hips. Both of them played a significant role in shaping me as a person. My grandmother was the one who had saved me in 1932 from the jaws of death.

Most Revered Gandhiji

During my illness in 1932, when my grandmother was looking after me, she used to tell me about Gandhiji of whom she was a great admirer. She had told me that God had sent

Gandhiji as his emissary to free India from British rule. She would narrate to me the innumerable brave acts of Gandhiji. She also explained to me that if everyone plied the charkha, which even she did, the poor would have clothes. The poor in India were without clothes and food and thus hungry and destitute. With my limited knowledge of English in 1935, I used to sit early in the morning in the verandah waiting for the English daily—*The Tribune*—to be delivered. I would scan through the headlines of the paper to look for any news on Gandhiji; my grandfather would explain to me where Gandhiji was and also narrated the Mahatma's speeches to me.

Earlier, when Gandhiji was visiting Lahore, I had pleaded with my father to take me to the place where Gandhiji was delivering his speech. I was about 8 years old. I could have been hurt in the stampede of the crowd. Hence, my father picked me up and sat me on his shoulder. That was the first time in my life that I saw Gandhiji. I noticed that Gandhiji was wearing a minimum of clothes. From the fringe of the audience from where we saw him, we found that he was seated on the dais. He appeared very frail.

From *The Tribune* I also learnt that there was a paper called the *Harijan* that Gandhiji was publishing, and it used to be released every week. I made enquiries and was informed that it would cost 2 *annas* to buy it and if I purchased all the 4-5 editions in a month, I would have to spare 8-10 *annas* from my allowance of Rs. 2. After much hesitation and deliberation, beginning from 1936 I started buying all the editions and thus I was able to preserve copies of the *Harijan*. When I advanced in my studies of English language in school, I started enjoying the subject and understanding Gandhiji's thought process. I used to read Gandhiji's writings again and again till the depth of the meanings would sink in me. I used to be emotionally moved by what Gandhiji was doing, particularly for the poor. After reading one issue of the *Harijan* a number of times, I would give away the paper to my grandfather and wait eagerly for the next issue to arrive.

On 29 January 1948, accompanied by my friend, Bir Khanna, I attended the prayer meeting of Gandhiji, when I saw Gandhiji for the second time. He appeared to be a man of tremendous spiritual strength, who could move mountains.

When Gandhiji died on 30 January 1948, I cried profusely and my tears would not stop. I attended his funeral the next day.

My grandmother told me that Gandhiji was specially deputed by God. She also told me that after Gandhiji made us free, he was recalled by God for further instructions.

Gandhiji was the greatest human being of the 20th century and he made all Indians proud, wherever they were, because he was an Indian.

6
More Injuries and Illnesses

In 1933, I was struck by another illness, i.e., an infection of eczema. My mother Lajwati had this eczema. I was nine years old and did not have much resistance power. My mother used to teach me and prepare me to go to school; she would also serve me food at regular intervals during the day. I fell an easy prey to eczema, which covered my hands extending to all the fingers and their tips. Someone from the joint household had to volunteer to apply medicated lotion, as prescribed for my mother by Ludhiana Lady Medical College, twice a day and bandage my hand and separately my fingers. Since the bandage could get wet from the oozing eruptions, which often transpired at the height of the eczema infection, it necessitated special attention. I was under considerable pain. Somebody had to feed me, whenever I was hungry, and hold a glass (tumbler) in their hands as I felt the need to drink water frequently. I required attention full-time, particularly when I cried out of pain.

When the situation became difficult, my grandmother took charge of me again, as she had done a year earlier when I had small pox.

I shifted to her part of the house. She looked after me with great love and affection. She ensured that the lotion would be applied more frequently. She got me a small bed, which used to lie next to her large bed. It took three months for the oozing eruptions to come under control and to be healed. I again missed school for the period that I was not well; further, this was also a preventive measure as there was a fear that if I attended school, the infection, which was contagious, could spread to the other boys in school.

My recovery was another triumph for Ammaji. It proved how much she cared for me.

The Tale of My Tricycle

In 1934, I injured my scalp. A doctor had to stitch a number of wounds. I was unconscious and post the injury, I had to lie in bed for a number of days. This was the last time that I had used my tricycle from my childhood days. Actually, the government had cut off water supply from municipal taps. Everyone was rushing to private wells to secure supplies. I put a metal bucket, which was filled with water, on one side of the handle and then pushed the tricycle right up to the maximum point from where it could slowly slide down. The tricycle, loaded on one side, was unable to bear the weight when I made an effort to pull it down. As a result, it turned upside down on me, leaving me unconscious and seriously injuring my scalp resulting in blood splashing all over my body. My father rushed me to a doctor, who applied stitches while I was unconscious.

When I regained consciousness, I remembered the rhyme:

Jack and Jill went up to the hill to fetch a pail of water. Jack fell down and broke his crown and Jill came tumbling after.

I never saw my tricycle again.

7
Life in Lahore: 1935-1940

In 1935, I told my father that I would not study further in the Sanatan Dharam School, as there were no proper chairs or desks and we were required to sit on coir mats. My father was comfortable with the idea. However, his only concern was the distance. D.A.V. School was about 4 miles away from where we lived, i.e., in Gwal Mandi (Market of Cows). Furthermore, he had reservations how I would adjust to a Hindi medium school without any extra tuitions to improve my linguistic skills in Hindi.

When I had arrived from Multan in 1930, I would sit on the lap of my grandmother while she would read aloud the *Bhagvad Gita* by Swami Satyanand. In due course, I learnt to distinguish different words and started pointing out to her whenever she missed a word or a letter; or, I would turn the page when I knew she was about to finish the last sentence of the page.

Before I shifted to D.A.V. School, she brought for me a book on the Hindi alphabet and explained to me how to construct sentences or write names. I distinctly remember demonstrating my writing skills to my father before I shifted to the D.A.V. School. Once I commenced my studies in school, I could carry out the shopping errands only on holidays and in my spare time.

The Dayal Singh Library was not very far from where we lived. I started spending a lot of time in reading books in English. These were mostly stories, fairytales and tales from lives of great men, which fascinated me a great deal. I was a regular visitor at the library until 1938 when we shifted to Krishan Nagar in Lahore.

In 1938, my grandfather built a house for us in Krishan Nagar, Lahore, not very far from where he had built one for himself.

Besides the Hindi language, I also began learning English up till 1938 with my grandfather. My grandfather had read upto matriculation level in Dera Ghazi Khan where he lived at that time but did not appear in the final exams. I familiarized myself with the English alphabet by sitting next to my grandfather who read *The Tribune* (the English daily) published from Lahore. My grasp of the language soon began to improve. This was my foundation of the English language.

Though I usually scored high grades in school during my entire school life, I never took special pains to excel and secure a higher rank in the class.

In 1940, I passed my matriculation examination, having failed to rank among the first 50 students in the university as I had taken up drawing as one of the subjects, which did not leave me with much of an option to score.

Sometime in 1933 or so, my father joined Hansraj Mahila Mahavidalaya, an exclusive women's college, under the control of D.A.V. College Management Committee. His salary was Rs. 35 per month.

When I was studying in the 9th standard, I informed my father that the school headmaster, Lala Suraj Bhan had offered me to contest the school election to be the school captain. Pitted against me was Rajender Sachar (who became the Chief Justice of the Delhi High Court), whose father, Lala Bhimsen Sachar, was at that time a leader of the Congress Party and who, subsequently, held the office of the Chief Minister of Punjab in independent India. My father cautioned me that I would definitely lose the election, because I belonged to an ordinary family with no political backing. His prediction came true—I lost the school election by 23 votes.

However, to compensate for the defeat, I began to excel in studies. In my final years at school, I was declared the all-round Best Boy. A huge teakwood polished board was placed in the Common Hall on which the names of outstanding students were inscribed. In this scroll of honour, my name appeared first. In addition, I received more than ten prizes on the annual prize distribution of the school.

My Grandfather: 'Babaji'

My grandfather, Lala Dayal Chand (Babaji), retired from Bharat Insurance Company Limited, Lahore in 1931. He, along with a colleague, had founded the company in 1894. In appreciation of their services, the founder chairman, Lala Harkishan Lal, assured them that the company would pay both of them life pension. Seth Ram Kishan Dalmia, who acquired control of the company from Lala Harkishan Lal, was reported to be hesitant in thinking whether he was bound by that understanding. As a result of a court case, my grandfather was awarded life pension of Rs. 90 per month being one-third of his salary of Rs. 270 per month, which he was drawing before his retirement. When in 1935, I took the decision to shift to D.A.V. Middle School, Lahore, which was 3-4 miles away from our residence-Gwal Mandi, my grandfather told my father that I should be able to eat something during the lunch interval of half an hour and buy *kulcha* (a type of flattened bread) with cooked gram costing two paise from the school Tuck Shop. My father with his monthly income of Rs. 35 was not able to afford any payment to me. We lived in a joint family under the supervision and control of my grandfather, who decided to give me pocket money of Rs. 2 per month. This would allow me to afford to pay 2 paise per day for the Tuck Shop and the 2 paise cost of sharing the *tonga* along with other minor boys making a total of 8 students for our return journey home in the evening. The *tonga driver* would thus get 4 *annas* (1/4th of a rupee).

8

Lahore High Court

I was in Class 6 of D.A.V. Middle School, Lahore. The year was 1936. I could see my father from a distance. He was dressed for a visit with Shri Mool Raj, the headmaster of our school. After a few minutes, the headmaster crossed the courtyard and came towards my class. This raised alarm signals in my mind whether everything was alright at home. The class stood up in salutation to the headmaster. The teacher called my name and asked me to pack up for the day, as my father had come to fetch me.

As we were walking out of the school, my father told me about the purpose of his visit. His friend Karuna Shankar Bhai from Kausindra, Gujarat, was here in Lahore. He told me that, Karuna Bhai desired to see me. "When we were living in Kausindra, you were a small child. You used to crawl about in their house. He remembers you distinctly," said my father.

Karuna Shankar was on a visit to Lahore as a part of a delegation led by Kanahiya Lal Munshi—a senior jurist and a distinguished lawyer. Munshi was an important man in India, who was going to argue the case of *The Tribune* before the Lahore High Court later that day.

Karuna Uncle was sitting in the car waiting for us. We would together witness the court hearing that day. Karuna Uncle gave me a tight hug, kissed my forehead and while putting his hands on my shoulders, said in broken Hindi: "How big our boy has grown. I would now take him away."

There was a separate gallery for visitors in the courtroom, Karuna Uncle, my father and I took the front seats that were allotted to us.

Two silver liveried men in red tunics made their appearance. They made the announcement that the court was in session. At this juncture, all those present in the courtroom stood up when two English judges wearing identical black long coats arrived and took their seats. Once the judges were seated, we all sat down and the proceedings of the court case began. I could not clearly understand all the arguments as the case was argued mostly in English all day long, and my knowledge of English while studying in the 6th standard in D.A.V. Middle School, Lahore, was very limited and sketchy. Nevertheless, I enjoyed watching the proceedings in the court.

9
D.A.V. College, Lahore: 1940-1944

The year was 1940. In those days, 'hazing' or 'ragging' (as it is described in South Asia) was a polite and courteous rite of passage and did not involve the bullying, almost torture, of new students.

On the first day when newcomers entered D.A.V. College, Lahore, a declamation contest was held in the common assembly hall of the college. The speaker was given a choice between two subjects after stepping on the podium. He had to complete an extempore speech in three minutes on any one of the subjects given to him. The senior students pursuing M.A. and the other higher classes also participated. The best speaker was to be awarded a cash prize of Rs. 50.

I was called upon to be the first speaker and was given two choices: "A well dressed man is a gentleman" or "Women are a nuisance to society".

I chose the second subject. After many students had spoken, some could not utter a single sentence due to stage fright. The jury pronounced its verdict in my favour.

In my intermediate year, I opted for Medical Science but due to paucity of marks I could not qualify in the open general list to join the Edward Medical College in Lahore.

For my graduation I chose Economics (Honours) as my principal subject besides Political Science, English Literature and one Indian or foreign language (as an optional subject), making a total of four subjects. The total marks obtained in all the four subjects determined one's rank and grade.

At the annual prize distribution of the college in 1944, I was invited to receive six prizes. The Principal made a citation to award me a gold medal for my performance in Political Science in B.A. (Honours) Economics final exams.

Military Engineering Services in Quetta (1942)

Here, I wish to make a brief mention of my maternal grandparents, uncles and aunts. I was born at Quetta in Baluchistan (now in Pakistan) on 4 July 1924, from which province my mother, Lajwati, hailed. My grandfather Lala Dasu Ram who was Tehsildar of Sibi and called "Nanaji" by us died in 1934. Our maternal grandmother Shanti Devi called "Biji" by us died in 1944 while she was living with us in Lahore. Uncle Rai Sahib Hon. Major Puran Chand Virmani, MBE, Masi Bhagwati; Uncle Lala Suraj Bhan, Advocate and Masi Dayawati. From 1932 onwards, it became a practice that I would visit Quetta and stay with one of my uncles. This routine was interrupted in 1935 when a severe earthquake hit the region. However, I resumed my visits from 1938 onwards until 1946.

In 1942, I was on a three-month holiday in Quetta. The British Army was looking for someone who could help the Commandant of Military Engineering Services and who could work as one of his personal assistants. Stalingrad was at that time under siege by the German forces. The Soviets, who were defending the city, were urgently in need of fuel, food, railway tracks, motor trucks, heavy machinery, guns and ammunition to keep the battle going. According to the then war plans of the Allied Forces, led by the United States, they would fortify Quetta if Stalingrad fell in German hands. For this purpose, a three-pronged policy was evolved; one, that all supplies needed for the defence of Stalingrad were to be made available from the base of Quetta. Further, the defences of Quetta were to be shored up, and reinforcement kept in the rear, in the event of Quetta becoming the theatre of war. On my agreeing to take up a temporary three-month assignment, I started working under the Commandant, reporting directly to him as his personal assistant.

The most rewarding and educative aspect of this assignment turned out to be access to dispatches from the headquarters in Delhi and how in real terms the Allies were facing the precarious situation in different theatres of war. I came to understand many facets about the conduct of the war.

Unfortunately, the road that the convoys took to rush supplies to Stalingrad was inhabited by hostile tribes. There was evidence of knocked out British tanks when I saw these wreckages on my return journey to Lahore. I had to take the same route as the convoys because the River Indus was severely flooded and the train and road routes to Lahore, had been snapped. On my return to Lahore I rested at Dera Ghazi Khan where I also had a chance to visit my ancestral home.

10
Dawn of Corruption and Debate on Partition

Dawn of corruption preceded the dawn of independence. The Second World War (1939 to 1945) resulted in the Indian subcontinent (South Asia) being converted as a base, where huge amounts had been pumped to thwart the advance of the Axis powers. In the East, Burma and Nicobar Islands were in occupation of the Japanese forces. They were knocking at the eastern flank of India. Their threat was real. The American Eastern Command (covering inter alia India and the East Indies) had prepared plans how to thwart the Japanese advance. On the western side, with the expected fall of Stalingrad, Quetta was the nerve centre from where plans were prepared to meet the German advance, should Stalingrad fall. Railway tracks were uprooted, petrol was being supplied and ammunition was being rushed to the Soviet forces defending Stalingrad. Any master plan for the defence of India had to convert the country into a fortress. Advance air strips were being built in accordance with the anticipated thrust of the enemy. To ensure war supplies to the likely theatres of war, roads were being laid. Many new cantonments with their infrastructures were ordered to be constructed. Everywhere round-the-clock activities were ushered in. This is where huge amounts were being paid to contractors. In all these hush-hush war preparations, quality standards were sacrificed. To state the facts, the contractors and army officers who passed the bills were paying least attention to correct certification of amounts. Both the parties pocketed large amounts of monies. To compound the problems of Allied Command in India, Gandhiji gave his call of Quit India at the top of the war crisis, which added to the atmosphere of uncertainty which is characteristic of a war psychosis. There was a large scale recruitment of armed forces. The Allied Command had moved the required scales of foreign troops to India. There were Italian and German prisoners of war who had been moved to India. Import of essential supplies into India was not possible. The available stocks were in short supply. Ration of wheat, rice and sugar was enforced to ensure priority supplies to armed forces. Those who had money were prepared to pay high prices for all items in short supply. This laid the foundation of inflation against the background of low prices in a decade of falling prices, that is, 1929-1939, which were the depression years. Salaried employees were started being paid dearness allowances to partially offset the effect of rising prices.

Government officers were willing partners in passing bogus supply bills and sub-standard constructions, which resulted in piles of unaccounted money in the hands of a new class of officers and all types of contractors. When the war commenced, the military started identifying contractors and when the war was half way through in 1942, they had developed a preference for contractors they wanted to deal with, which gave birth to corrupt practices.

At some military stations, there was a need for daily supply of milk, workforce, tailors, vegetables, fruits and meat suppliers, and shopkeepers who would sell groceries. The government had forfeited stocks of wheat, rice and sugar, petrol, cement and steel for which they had introduced rationing for the urban civilian population. Coupons for petrol on need-based basis were issued on the nature of profession of motor car owners. Carpenters and mechanics on stand-alone basis or in groups were hired. For certain theatres of war like the Middle East and the Soviet Union, India was making identifiable supplies. The country had become a big workshop functioning round the clock. Those who made supplies and worked for the government had to be paid. As the momentum of war grew, uncertainties of future took shape and with it the moral fibre of the nation deteriorated. Some of the officers who were authorized to make payments felt that some part of the money should come to them. Similarly, some of those officers making supplies to the military machine took to cheating the government by making under supplies and for work done and not done or not fully done. Some of these aforesaid officers who were working for the government joined hands in openly accepting bribes for receiving under supplies and less work. During the war, this became a malpractice of looting the government through all possible means and all involved unjustly enriched themselves. This was chapter one of the dawn of corruption.

The second area of corruption was provided by rationing —wheat, rice, sugar, petrol and cement. These were grey areas in which the black market flourished. These were the items for which the needy were prepared to pay the market price and, thus, an underground market flourished. In this way, as the war gathered momentum, the black market grew in size and in speed. This was in open violation of Defence of India Rules. People who made supplies of essential commodities often at 100 per cent more than the price fixed by the government, in open defiance of law to make money, was another form of corruption. This market flourished for a number of years after independence.

During the war years and thereafter, the trading community and those engaged in different types of goods needed for human consumption made enormous profits, which they applied in buying the shares of many enterprises owned by those British industrial interests who were reluctantly leaving India. These foreign enterprises fell into the hands of the rich Indian community. They could not be managed with the same degree of discipline, efficiency and strict application of rules and procedures necessary for their healthy growth. In this atmosphere, the bureaucrats, without any knowledge or expertise, issued more clumsy and inappropriate outlines as to how these sinking enterprises should be managed, making confusion worse confounded.

The dawn of corruption laid down the psyche of what actual corruption would be like. It started to take away the fear of breaking established laws and practices. It showed a way how officers could be influenced through bribes. The methods used during the war of under supply and over charging were misused in the imports and exports business in independent India. This misuse perfected corruption and laid the foundation for the future accumulation of black money at both the national and international levels. Through the medium of national black money, huge assets in real estate, bullion, and industrial and trading empires were set up. The Income Tax Department was unaware of the details of this black money at the time of its inception. Money laundering came into being and India was no exception. Chapter XXV conveys my thoughts on black money, which I may also describe as 'Black Money India International'.

Debate on Partition—Government College, Lahore

Before I left the D.A.V. College, Principal G.L. Dutta nominated me to participate in a debate, the subject of which was 'The partition of India is not in the interest of the country.' I had to defend the proposition while the speaker from the Government College, Lahore was to oppose me. The time allotted was 15-20 minutes to each speaker. I had the right to reply and the proposition was to be put to vote. My father discussed the issue with me for a number of days.

I opened the debate, which was held in the winter of 1943-44, in the hall of the Government College, Lahore. Initiating the debate I said that Gandhi and Jinnah were children of the same renaissance movement. The pride of these two great men was hurt to find India in slavery. They might have had different points of view, but both were great fighters for India's freedom and were genuine patriots. I had not concluded the last sentence when suddenly there was a great commotion in the hall. A large group from the audience rushed to the stage and started shouting at me with slogans of 'Pakistan Zindabad' and 'Quaid-e-Azam Jinnah Zindabad'. I spoke to the person who was shouting the most that I had not said a word about Pakistan. He replied that I must address Jinnah as Quaid-e-Azam Jinnah. Suddenly my eyes fell on the far end of the hall, where I found my father trying to get up and come to the dais. I signalled to him not to leave his seat. I consented to address Jinnah as Quaid-e-Azam. I had prepared my case for debate, based entirely on social, cultural and economic factors. The burden of my speech was that Muslims were being discriminated on economic issues and in senior government jobs. They needed to be given better opportunities in the economic and educational fields. Historically, the emperors of Delhi, throughout the Islamic rule, wanted the whole of undivided India under their control. So had the British. Independent India would benefit from one unified country as it had the same ethos, and we thought and spoke on the same wavelength. We were children of the same ancestors. We were bound by the same bonds of blood. A common thread of culture and customs ran through our veins. How could momentary misunderstandings be the cause of our separation? There was no other disturbance and I continued the debate, though without any cheers at the end of my speech.

The essential points in the speech of the speaker who opposed me in the debate were that the Hindus had not treated Muslims with equality or respect. According to him,

Muslims drew their inspiration from their holy book—the *Qu'ran*. He added that Muslims were self-respecting people. They felt that it was impossible to live with Hindus any longer. He proclaimed that nothing could stop the formation of the separate Islamic State based on the *Shari'a*. He assured the audience that Pakistan would be the land of the pure. Hindus, Sikhs and Christians would be treated as brothers and sisters and every Muslim would be duty-bound to protect their dignity and honour after Pakistan came into being (he was loudly cheered at this stage). He concluded his speech by raising the slogan 'Pakistan Zindabad' and 'Quaid-e-Azam Jinnah Zindabad'. The proposition was put to vote and the Nayes had it. The Principal of the Government College asked me if I wanted to respond to the debate. Instead, I walked up to the speaker who opposed me, I praised him and shook hands with him for his excellent speech. There were loud cheers and the debate was concluded.

11
Career with PNB, Lahore and Partition and Independence of India

I secured a job with the Punjab National Bank Ltd. at their head office in Lahore in October 1944. The bank offered me to start as a junior clerk. Due to my family's precarious financial position, I accepted the offer. The Punjab National Bank Ltd. (PNB) had 282 branches in undivided India as a whole but its concentration was mostly in the north of India, with nearly one-third of the branches (91) falling within the borders of future Pakistan. It is also noteworthy that Bombay, Calcutta, Madras, Karachi, Rangoon and practically all important trading and industrial towns had single or multiple branches. I had been assigned the task of processing credit proposals from 15–20 branches. The overall control of the loans and advances department, comprising about 50 people, vested with the Superintendent, Thakur Mool Singh.

About a year after joining the bank, Thakur Mool Singh asked me if on every Sunday or a bank holiday, I could visit his house to help him dispose of those files where further investigation and understanding were needed. He wanted me to go through such files. On my visit to his house, I explained to him the crux of the problem and based on further enquiries, clarifications and assessments, he made up his mind and passed the necessary orders. I welcomed this opportunity because I came to know the names, nature of dealings and types of industries and businesses being carried out by the borrowers from all over the country. PNB had customers among major business houses. The bank had large resources (11 per cent of the country's bank deposits, excluding imperial and foreign banks); it was professionally managed; it offered first class service; and it had a disciplined, courteous and well-trained staff. For about a year and a half, I cycled to his house with files tied to the carrier of my cycle. This exercise helped me to get an idea of the famous business houses and their owners. Thakur Mool Singh also enlightened me further on the background of the businessmen.

On 1 April 1947, Thakur Mool Singh called me and gave me a note, comprising the draft of a letter prepared by Lala Yodhraj, Chairman, General Manager and majority shareholder of the bank, to be dispatched to all those branches of the Bank (estimated at that time at 97) likely to fall in Pakistan. The letter began with M.A. Jinnah declaring the creation of Pakistan, if necessary by the sword. As the bank was a trustee of the depositors, we were duty-bound to protect their interests. Lala Yodhraj foresaw large-scale violence, arson, looting and dislocation of life, business and people. Instructions were, therefore, being issued to all the branch managers whose branches were likely to fall under Pakistan, stating no further drawings be allowed by way of fresh advances. Borrowers were informed of the cancellation of their credit limits and all the borrowers, except those who had drawn against their own deposits, were called upon to forthwith liquidate their accounts. Their stocks and securities, which were under the bank's physical control and custody, would be sold after due notice. A daily report would be sent to the head office marked to the attention of recovery section regarding the progress concerning the liquidation of loans and advances and the transfer of depositors' funds. Further, a duplicate copy of all daily transactions, called the daybook, would be sent to the bank's Nagpur branch in India, to protect the interests of the depositors and to ensure that in the event of the total destruction of records, there would be some evidence about the movement of accounts. Apart from the daybook, duplicate certified true copies of all other connected relevant documents would also be sent to the Nagpur branch in suitable identifiable dockets. I was relieved of my other routine responsibilities. This was the only assignment which I had to undertake and discharge to the best of my ability, even if it meant working on all holidays and late at night.

In the two-and-a-half years since October 1944 when I joined the bank, I was promoted at a relatively quick pace. On the day this work was assigned to me, I was on probation as a senior accountant.

In compliance with the instructions to the branches, I started receiving a daily report citing the relevant status of deposits and advances with a confirmation that a copy of the same along with a copy of the daybook had been sent to Nagpur.

Partition and Independence of India
(15 August 1947)

There are tomes written on the partition of India in August 1947 and the independence that India eventually achieved on 15 August 1947 from the British rule. The partition of India has been one of the most significant, yet tragic and traumatic events in Indian history. I, too, witnessed this agonizing period in our country's history.

Mahatma Gandhi, the architect of India's freedom, has been affectionately called 'Bapu', the father of the nation. Pandit Jawaharlal Nehru, the first prime minister of independent India, and Sardar Vallabhai Patel were also among the pivotal and prominent figures in India's independence struggle. Mahatma Gandhi, the towering giant of the 20th century, stands tall and relevant even today. Gandhiji's thinking and writings are the balm that can heal the world of its troubles and tragedies.

PNB, LAHORE (AUGUST 1947)

As we entered the month of August in 1947, I was shocked to find that by the end of the first week, there were no executives, officers, clerks or any other member of subordinate staff available in the bank. With the exception of some Muslim watchmen and ward staff, all non-Muslim staff members had apparently left Lahore or they were making arrangements to do so.

I used to walk up to the General Post Office, which was right opposite the bank. I would collect mail and telegrams. Most of the telegrams were in code and after decoding them, I made the necessary entries in the register.

I shifted my grandparents, parents, my aunts and their children to a refugee camp (converted from the D.A.V. College hostel) having removed most of our possessions from our respective houses. I shifted heavy items to the bank in my room in the hope that they would remain safe. The shops were closed and roads were deserted, as most of the areas were under curfew. I somehow managed to attend the office until the end of August. I continued to stay with my grandparents and parents in the refugee camp. The means of communication between Lahore and the head office of the bank, which had by then shifted its registered office to New Delhi with prior permission of the Lahore High Court in May, 1947, could not be established. Some remote branches in Pakistan continued to send their daily reports to me. Once those branches also stopped functioning, I decided to visit New Delhi to seek further instructions. When I left Pakistan, I still hoped that we would return to our homeland and re-occupy our house. I travelled via Ferozepur and reached Delhi by or about in the middle of September 1947, as it took seven to ten days to reach Delhi from Ferozepur since the train connections were so badly affected. I managed to contact Thakur Mool Singh and conveyed to him whatever latest information I had. I gave him, based on the latest data, my estimate of the losses the bank would incur. The information was conveyed to the Chairman and other senior executives. A few months post partition, Thakur Mool Singh passed away. I reported for duty at the head office for further orders, as my assignment tenure in Lahore, had, in effect ended.

Problems in PNB Head Office Post Partition

There was great pressure from refugees who had taken shelter in different parts of India, as they began to demand the return of their deposits. Those who had taken the bank's advice to transfer these deposits and operational accounts to India faced no problems, but the vast majority did not anticipate that all Hindus and Sikhs would be forced to leave the country of their ancestors.

In order to restore confidence and to make available immediate funds to the refugees, a counterpart of every branch in Pakistan on its own or as a part of a cluster of branches was opened at convenient locations. Documents from Nagpur listing movements of daily transactions became handy. However, it was not clear if that was the last dispatch. In any case, based on identification, and some proof that clients had dealings with the respective branch, within a matter of a few weeks, the rehabilitation operation of refugees who were customers of PNB was in full swing. There were Muslim depositors who continued to live in Pakistan as well as Muslim refugees and customers of the PNB who migrated from India. Their problems were more complicated. The branches which had closed in Pakistan had all the relevant records but there was no one to service the clients. The migrants from India too had records in India but again no one to service them in Pakistan. When the picture was finally drawn up, the Muslims constituted 10 to 15 per cent of PNB's customer base.

Before the end of August 1947, all branches of the PNB in Pakistan had ceased to function. Ninety per cent of the branches in Pakistan, though shuttered, remained unaffected barring arson and break-in attempts at a few Pakistani branch offices.

The governments of India and Pakistan arrived at an agreement, so that we could take possession of our records, and allowed two branches of PNB to function in Pakistan. The problem of customers who had boxes in safe deposit vaults was solved, as they were allowed access to remove their possessions under police/military escort. Within one year, after partition, all outstanding issues concerning banking operations were resolved.

In order to rehabilitate about 2000 employees who had been uprooted from the branches in Pakistan, the Reserve Bank of India gave PNB a blanket permission to open 60 branches in India.

Notwithstanding the best efforts that the bank had made in opening new branches, absorbing all the surplus staff from Pakistan in the new branches and also deploying them in the existing branches, giving at the same time the best customer service we could render to the people displaced from Pakistan, there appeared to be an undercurrent of unease how a bank, which had one-third of its branches in Pakistan accounting for 50 per cent of its business from the displaced residents of West Pakistan, could survive the disastrous effects, which almost every refugee coming from West Pakistan had suffered.

The senior management of the bank, which oversaw the institution on a day-to-day basis, conveyed to the public that the bank was financially and structurally sound. In terms of management and customer service, it was one of the best banks in the country. The public, however, nursed a sense of uncertainty and had a gnawing feeling that there was something amiss and the bank was trying to conceal the truth from the public.

12
Run on the Punjab National Bank Ltd (1949)

On the failure of Exchange Bank of India and Africa Ltd. in Kenya in April-May 1949, we were informed that there were rumours in the Bombay market that PNB was not a sound institution and that it could be a victim of a possible run on the bank. As the rumours gathered momentum, panic broke out in Bombay by the second week of May 1949, and it was found that people were standing in queues to withdraw their savings from the bank. At that time, the liquidity of the bank was sound. The bank had deposits of Rs. 60 crores. PNB accounted for 10-11 per cent share in deposits excluding deposits of Imperial Bank and foreign banks. PNB's investments in government securities amounted to over Rs. 31 crores and it had cash in hand to the tune of Rs. 8 crores. Thus, PNB's commitment in loans and advances amounted to Rs. 23 crores only, which was a low figure. The total paid up capital and reserves were over Rs. 1 crore.[1]

While the run in Bombay had not peaked, the main assault of depositors occurred in Delhi, where PNB had the

---

[1] Extracted from the accounts of the Punjab National Bank in the 1947 Balance Sheet, which are public documents.

largest network of nearly 20 branches. The larger concentration of affluent people living in West Pakistan had re-located to Delhi. Within a matter of two days, the entire nation had been engulfed by this crisis of confidence. The strategy adopted uniformly all over the country was that the bank had stopped doing all other types of business and was prepared to pay up in full, the entire amount lying in the current, savings and fixed deposit accounts with interest calculated where applicable, up to date.

In order to first meet the mounting demand for cash, the bank pledged all of its government securities with the Reserve Bank of India. On the penultimate day before the run, some executives and I went to Lala Yodhraj's house and told him that having exhausted all the resources, there was a lot of money lying with branches which could not be used for fear of immediate demand.

One strategy that evolved that evening was that at every branch at Delhi where the crisis of confidence was the maximum, there should be a parallel line of the bank's own staff and other well-wishers who should carry cash (to be given by the bank to them) and, insist on the bank manager to take the money back as the run on the bank was ill-founded. It could have two effects: it would slow down the withdrawals because the cashiers would start taking back the deposits, and, psychologically people would have a sense of assurance that as other depositors were putting the money back and there was danger of keeping cash at home, it was better to leave the money with the bank.

A team of the bank, which would be taking care of those customers to re-deposit the money, was organized by the bank. Those who had come to withdraw the money were outnumbered by those who wanted to deposit their funds. As the news of the run having come to an end spread round the country, genuine customers also returned and began depositing, if not all, at least a part of the amount that was earlier withdrawn.

As far as the order of precedence was concerned, until I left the bank in 1956, I continued to be ranked as the junior most among the group of people who participated in decision-making meetings. In 1950, I was provided with an office car and an addition in my emoluments was made through the medium of compensatory allowances, a furnished house and other perks and privileges, and I was designated as Public Relations Officer. However, I always had direct access to different levels of executives. In particular, I developed mutual trust and confidence with the Chairman and General Manager Lala Yodhraj.

Helping in the Formation of King's Union

One day, sometime in the autumn of 1949, Lala Yodhraj called me to check if I could accompany him as he wanted to discuss an important matter. He appeared concerned that the Communist Party of India had started a union in the bank. His explained that although he was not against unions or the bank having a union affiliated to the Communist Party, his only worry was that the Communist Party had not accepted that India had attained independence. They considered Pandit Jawaharlal Nehru to be a 'lackey' of imperialist powers, led by the United States of America.

They were leading an armed uprising in Telangana (then a part of Hyderabad and now a separate State) in the hope that they would be able to overthrow the government in New Delhi; it seemed they were taking instructions from Moscow. The Communist Party of India was a part of an international movement called 'Comintern'.

Lala Yodhraj felt that the Communists would try to organise unions in banking, insurance, railways, textile mills, tea gardens and jute mills to strangulate India economically and make India a part of the Soviet Bloc. While PNB was financially sound, and structurally ones of them best in the country communists through their proxy unions could create problems of fear, lack of confidence and try to disrupt the smooth economy of the country in which the PNB had come to assume a critical role.

I told Lala Yodhraj that since the Communists had already taken the initiative of forming a union in the bank, I suggested the formation of another union. This would essentially be a tactical move to keep the communists engaged in fighting a rival union. I was inspired by Sardar Vallabhai Patel's strategy of initiating a rival All-India Trade Union Organisation called Indian National Trade Union Congress (INTUC), a rival union which could be independent of all other formations that could be formed in the bank.

Within a short period, the 'King's' Union, called 'Punjab National Bank Workmen's Union' was registered. Subsequently, a meeting was called at Lala Yodhraj's office where all branch managers in Delhi and some executives were invited. At the head office, a meeting was organised which was presided and directed by Lala Yodhraj where he distributed blank forms seeking membership of the union to the branch managers and heads of departments, who were further instructed by Lala Yodhraj to get the forms filled by clerical and subordinate staff and to send the forms to me by the evening of the following day. As General Secretary of the union, I immediately applied to the Chief Labour Commissioner that over 800 members had formed a union. I signed the letter as General Secretary, requesting the government to recognize the union as the majority outfit. There was an irony in the scheme of things that I was an officer trying to run a clerical union. No one seemed concerned about these legal niceties. The sympathy of the vast majority of staff was with the original communist union. At its very optimum number, the PNB Workmen's Union in Delhi could claim genuine membership of 70-80 persons only.

The working committee of the PNB Workmen's Union started meeting regularly demanding improvement in working conditions, regularization of pay scales, better quality uniforms, and coolers at different branches in the summer months. The management accepted all the demands.

Simultaneously, steps were taken to enlarge the scope of activities of the union by laying stress on positive and constructive methods of functioning. The following activities were initiated to divert the attention of the staff to the positive aspect of things:

(a) A study circle was formed where eminent men, economists and government dignitaries were invited to address the study circle proceedings, which were open to the members of the staff of all ranks.

(b) A cultural wing encouraging music, drama, songs, skits and poetry reading was also started.

(c) Baisakhi day, the foundation day of the bank, which fell every year on 13 April, was celebrated with great pomp and show where ministers and eminent personalities were invited as chief guests.

(d) A cooperative store, which sold essential commodities at discounted rates, was opened. Under the then prevailing government rules, the members of the co-operative store were entitled to receive items in short supply at concessional rates. Arrangements were also made to supply heavy and major grocery items (if the purchases were large) at the residence of a member of the store.

(e) I was appointed Editor of the PNB Staff Monthly News. After I took over as economic advisor in 1952, I started a weekly economic news bulletin, of which I was appointed the Editor.

Though efforts were made to extend the membership of the Workmen's Union across the country, these only met with partial success. The members of the 'King's' Union, were some of the best employees who continued to serve the cause of the union with utmost sincerity. They endured insults, humiliations, social boycott and other indignities, but never swerved from the path they had chosen by joining the Workmen's Union. Long after I left the bank, a few continued to remain in touch with me until I left the country for a long spell.

CALL OF STRIKE IN PNB

The pro-communist PNB Employees' Union wanted to expand its sphere of influence and to achieve this goal, it deputed one M.L. Sabharwal to proceed to Bombay and organise the Bombay-based union on strong and effective lines. He applied for leave, which was rejected, but in violation of the order rejecting his leave, Sabharwal proceeded to Bombay. Upon his return, he was suspended from service. As a consequence, the employees in Delhi went on a pen down strike. The Employees' Union gave a call for an all India strike, and about 5,000 workers out of nearly 6,000 employees of the PNB went on strike in April 1951.

The strike and its countrywide impact were discussed at length between the then Prime Minister Pandit Jawaharlal Nehru and Lala Yodhraj. As narrated to me subsequently by Lala Yodhraj, the Prime Minister was livid. C.D. Deshmukh, the then Finance Minister, wanted an immediate resolution to the crisis as the Bank had terminated the services of all employees who continued to remain on strike.

Lala Yodhraj suggested that if 300 of the employees were kept out of the bank, pending the outcome of adjudication by a labour tribunal, he would let the other employees sitting on strike, resume their work. The Prime Minister felt that the number of suspended employees should not exceed more than 15-20. Lala Yodhraj declared that he would prefer to take the bank into voluntary liquidation and assured the Prime Minister that no depositor would lose any money. At this stage, Finance Minister Deshmukh advised the Prime Minister that the matter ought to be left between Lala Yodhraj and Deshmukh to further negotiate and settle the issue.

It was eventually agreed that 150 employees against whom the bank had substantive charges of misdemeanour should be suspended, and their cases would be settled by a labour tribunal. The rest of the striking employees could resume work if they so desired.

The events which have been referred to above eventually reached the Supreme Court of India. On 24 September 1959, a three-member bench of the Supreme Court delivered its final verdict. The Punjab National Bank Ltd. vs. its Workmen AIR 1960 160, 1960 SCR(1) 806.

Meeting Dr Gyan Chand

In 1949, I met Dr Gyan Chand, the famous Indian economist of the 1940s, at the residence of my father's friend in Delhi. Dr Gyan Chand told us that at that time he was updating the Prime Minister, Pandit Jawaharlal Nehru, in the wider context of the Indian economy as it might have undergone changes post the conclusion of the National Plan Committee deliberations, which Pandit Nehru had chaired in 1939–1940. The war years (1939–1945) could have brought new issues to the fore, which needed to be attended to urgently and Panditji wanted those problems to be listed on a priority basis. I mentioned to Dr Gyan Chand that I would be shortly completing five years of service in the PNB and had got involved in helping the management in resolving matters that affected the rehabilitation of refugees after the Partition of India. I also told him that banks should do something substantial by getting directly involved in providing funds towards the rapid economic development and industrialization of the country. Since Dr Gyan Chand was occupying a position from where he could positively influence the direction of the Government, I had been studying this aspect and wished to discuss the matter with him.

When I met Dr Gyan Chand in his well-furnished and impressive office in the annexes of the Governor General's estate (later Rashtrapati Bhavan), I told him that considering my limited exposure to the basics of banking, I was not competent to elaborate on what the country required to do to achieve rapid economic development and industrialization. However, during the last two years or so I was in-charge of the Bombay desk, which meant that all business proposals emanating from the Bombay branches were processed by me. I had also visited all important businesses, including trading houses and industries located in and around Bombay, in a period of more than two weeks and formed certain conclusions, which I said I wanted to share with him. The following are some of the brief points of my presentation to Dr Gyan Chand:

(i) The entrepreneurs, i.e., those who owned and managed their enterprises, had one objective—to make maximum profits from day-to-day activities. This was to be achieved by speculation, manipulation and by maintaining multiple books of accounts. A trader had no social conscience. In the war years (1939–1945), 20 new banks became operational. Practically all of them were floated and managed by traders, except New Bank of India Ltd., National Bank of Lahore Ltd., and Punjab & Sind Bank Ltd. At the time of my presentation to Dr Gyan Chand, all new ventures had collapsed after lingering around for 3 to 5 years.

(ii) There was misapplication and misutilization of deposits representing the nation's savings by promoting various types of new businesses of trading communities, who at the relevant time managed and commandeered the nation's banks. The resources of the country were not being applied for the development of enterprises including industries, which was the need of the hour for our country, which had recently gained independence.

(iii) The Government had to find a way so that the savings of the nation could be productively used for development purposes.

Dr Gyan Chand thanked me for my presentation and said that he would bring these essential points to the attention of the concerned people.

13
Mahatma Hansraj and My Association with Lala Yodhraj

My father, Professor Atmanand, who was a well-known figure in Arya Samaj circles, and a regular speaker at the various temples of the Arya Samaj both in Lahore and in Delhi, informed me in the year 1966 that he had been asked to speak on the life of Mahatma Hansraj. He asked me if I could speak to Lala Yodhraj so as to persuade him to shed some light on the life of his father (Mahatma Hansraj). At the time, I was living in Bombay whereas my father lived in Delhi. During one of my frequent meetings with Lala Yodhraj, the latter did enlighten me about Mahatma Hansraj. I sent a note dated 16 February 1966, to my father based on Lala Yodhraj's recollections of his father, a copy of which I kept with me and which is reproduced below:

> "Mahatma Hansraj did not allow DAV College section of Arya Samaj Movement to get associated or identified with Gandhiji's Movement. He appreciated and supported Gandhiji's programme of Harijan reform and widow remarriage as well as the spread of education. He either kept quiet or even opposed Gandhiji when he felt he was spreading disaffection against established order.

He felt that such activities of Gandhiji would undermine the strength of a strong and powerful India when India became free. He was prepared for India to get freedom but not at the expense of India compromising what he felt were basic requirements of persuading an individual to respect authority and discipline. His nationalism, secularism and love for the country were never in doubt. Muslims sent their children to DAV schools and colleges and no one ever accused him of having a communal bias. His sincerity of purpose was beyond reproach even when he was in the forefront of converting Muslims into Hindus, more particularly in the Agra Division. His physical endurance was put to severe test, when walking through villages, his feet had sore boils and burns. His actions never provoked hostility and this showed a special strength of his character, because he acted with clean hands, never minced words but never hurt anyone's feelings.

"Mahatma Hansraj never compromised on his self-respect. When his son Balraj was imprisoned, well-meaning intermediaries knowing the British mind told him that if he agreed to meet the Governor of Punjab, special consideration could be shown to his son. Mahatma Hansraj was never haughty or self-righteous. He told the friends of the rulers that he did not mean to hurt the feelings of his son or belittle his son's sacrifice by seeking an interview with the Governor.

"Mahatma Hansraj's wife, as a mother, however, felt that if Balraj could be saved, the father must do something. He just used to keep quiet and never discussed the question with any relatives and friends.

"When Yodhraj was in search of employment and later for a social status and identity, he (Mahatma Hansraj) never interfered in his activities nor ever allowed him (Yodhraj) to use his name or influence. Yodhraj used to say, how could one define or understand his father. He had a tremendous depth and no one could read from his face what was passing through his mind. He had learnt not only to master suffering, but even made a virtue of it.

"He had weak eye sight. Also he used to get high fevers. He never complained. He seldom had any money, not even in times of serious illness of his sons and daughters. He never informed anyone. He did not turn for help or assistance but nursed the sick ones himself; he never showed any emotion.

"People trusted him and went to him with their problems. He often gave money from his paltry salary (Rs. 45 per month), more so to teachers of the school and college where he worked. He never mentioned to anyone that he had given money nor would he accept any return of money even if it was understood to have loaned it or was himself in dire need.

"Just before he died, he told his brother Mulk Raj to stand near him so that he could see him properly before he breathed his last. Mulk Raj also wanted to know if he could place Rs. 4 lakh at the disposal of Mahatma Hansraj about which the latter could indicate how he wanted it to be spent. Mahatma Hansraj smiled and merely desired Mulk Raj to be within his sight as he breathed his last."

Mahatma Hansraj was born on 19 April 1864 and died on 15 November 1938. DAV College Trust and Managing Society was registered on 16 August 1886. In 1914-15 Balraj was tried at Delhi, charged with murder and for being a member of the underground Revolutionary movement of Rash Behari Bose and after trial he was convicted to life imprisonment. On appeal the sentence was reduced to 7 years imprisonment in place of transportation for life.

Mahatma Hansraj was a visionary with great foresight, a selfless leader with exceptional qualities, a true social reformer who will be remembered for generations to come.

Mahatma Hansraj's influence was so powerful that the DAV School/College Movement started in 1886 still continues to grow and has over 715 schools and colleges and other technical training institutes spread in different parts of the country. These are either named after Swami Dayanand or Mahatma Hansraj and (they) teach modern technology English, Hinduism, dentistry, nursing and healthcare, with emphasis on English as a medium of instruction, where applicable. They continue to play a dominant role in various parts of the country. They are controlled, managed and mostly funded by DAV College Managing Committee, Headquarters in Delhi. Similarly, there is no city or town in urban North India which does not have an Arya Samaj where people assemble every week and perform Havan.

My Association with Lala Yodhraj

My association with Lala Yodhraj extended for 25 years from 1949 to 1975. When I went to different places but could not meet him, we carried on regular correspondence and remained in touch with each other. Lala Yodhraj quit his services at the Punjab National Bank Ltd. on 23 November 1953, by which time Seth Shanti Prasad Jain had assumed full control of the bank. Seth Shanti Prasad Jain first nominated his family member Seth Shriyans Prasad Jain as Chairman. A year later, he became the Chairman himself.

As we got closer, I found that Lala Yodhraj was getting more and more withdrawn into himself and looked forward to some company. During most of this period, i.e., 1956 onwards, I was working with the Central Bank of India and he had more or less fixed a programme in a manner that I would meet him, if possible every Saturday for lunch. Occasionally, accompanied by our wives we would watch a movie during weekends. We would also go for long walks while in Delhi at India Gate and at Marine Drive in Bombay or at his large house at Pali Hill in Bombay, and stayed on for dinner at his house in Pali Hill. On a few occasions, he would also visit us.

He had a photographic memory, a very large library and his interests extended to history, science, space, technology, wars, military affairs, economics and financial matters, discussions on various religions, sociology, and world affairs. Often when I met him after a week or a fortnight, or, as the occasion demanded, he had practically read another book and engaged me in discussion on the specific subject he had read. On some subjects he alone spoke but there would be quite a number of issues where I would participate in his discussions with me. On economic matters, my assessment and his views were often at variance, because he was in business while I had an overview of ground realities, as I was in active banking. For instance, he asked me to give him strong and weak points of his administration in PNB and my assessment of The Central Bank of India[1] Ltd. at that time.

I just replied to him in two sentences that his rule was authoritarian in PNB while Central Bank had a friendly, participative management with autonomy of action to different executives. After some deliberation, he told me that Bombay was a business town and the largest commercial centre in India, while Delhi was highly bureaucratic, and that should explain the difference in the styles of management.

I learnt a great deal from his clear thinking. He was a practical man and in a period of 10 years, during which he was the Executive Chairman and majority shareholder from 1943 to 1953 of PNB, he had changed the face of PNB from that of a localized provincial bank to an all India bank with a sizeable share in banking business, then available in the country.

In between 1949 to 1952, through my contacts with Sardar Pratap Singh Kairon and Lala Jagat Narain, who were stalwarts in the Punjab Congress and whom Lala Yodhraj had financially helped every now and then to get into seats of

---

[1] My tenure and work in The Central Bank of India Ltd., subsequently known as Central Bank of India, is described in subsequent chapters.

power, they both had persuaded the Prime Minister Pandit Jawaharlal Nehru to consider giving Lala Yodhraj a Congress nominee ticket in the 1952 elections. (My acquaintance with these two Congress leaders introduced me to the Congress culture.) However, one of our erstwhile teachers and a friend and a colleague in the bank, Captain A.N. Bali was an RSS worker, who persuaded Lala Yodhraj to contest the 1952 General Elections on the Jan Sangh ticket and put him up as a candidate from two constituencies from Punjab, i.e. Karnal and Kangra. The trends of the results were available to the Congress leaders while counting was going on. Pratap Singh Kairon telephoned me from Jalandhar saying that Lala Yodhraj was trailing behind and was going to lose heavily. On the retirement of Captain A.N. Bali, I succeeded him as the bank's Economic Adviser in 1952.

Lala Yodhraj was in his own time the top-most banker in the country, highly respected and an effective and strong speaker as well as a very powerful personality. He wanted to serve the country in an important capacity, but he had his weak points too. He was not very social and did not have the ability of being a political manipulator. In my long association with him, I did not come across any other person who was close to him. When I think of him in retrospect, I hold him in very high respect. I stayed and worked overseas for 23 years and after his death in 1975, I served many institutions and banks but could not find a person of his singular mental concentration and intellectual clarity.

Later on in his life, he developed bleeding ulcers. Though he had fully recovered but due to some wrong medication in

Canada in 1975, he suffered a severe setback and could not recover from that fatal illness; he passed away in Canada in 1975.

Lala Yodhraj was a mentor to me and I will always remain grateful for the friendship that we shared over the years during which it was my privilege to have worked with him and known him.

14
The Punjab National Bank Ltd: Dalmia-Jain Group

Immediately after the partition of the country, Seth Ram Krishan Dalmia, who was a leading businessman at the time, appeared to have taken the decision to persuade Lala Yodhraj (who was then the Chairman and General Manager of the PNB controlling 56 per cent shareholding of the bank through a trust called 'Ramsharnam Trust'), to sell PNB to him. Dalmia assured Lala Yodhraj that he would ensure that whatever happened to PNB on account of losses that it might have suffered due to the impact of Partition, he would support PNB and he was prepared to compensate Lala Yodhraj for a sum, which would be many times more than his original investment in the PNB. It appeared that Lala Yodhraj was reluctant to part with the control and management of PNB as he feared that his goodwill would suffer, and, that the family from which he came and the Punjabi community of which he was a respected member, would never forgive him if he sold the bank for whatever financial consideration Dalmia might pay him. Lala Yodhraj told him that he was not interested. Sometime later, Dalmia established contact with Lala Yodhraj stating that he was prepared to pay the price of the shares, leaving the control and management of the bank in the hands of Lala Yodhraj. (Lala Yodhraj yielded the control of the bank to Seth Shanti Prasad Jain, son-in-law of Seth Ram Krishan Dalmia in November 1953.)

My first clash with Seth Shanti Prasad Jain occurred when I was preparing for the Diamond Jubilee Celebrations of PNB scheduled to be held on 13 April 1955. Seth Shanti Prasad Jain asked me that when the draft of the history of the bank being prepared by me was ready, he should have a copy and nothing should be published without his consent. In due course of time, I sent the manuscript to him and this led to a stormy meeting between the two of us. In one sentence, his direction was that the history must be slanted to the glory and greatness of the Dalmia-Jain Group, as they were really the saviours and makers of the bank. I told him that I would invite his comments on the manuscript. His personal assistant, P. Subramanium, was sent the revised draft. After making additions and alterations, he deleted in entirety the major contribution of Lala Yodhraj covering a few pages. Lala Yodhraj's full-page photograph was to be reduced to passport size and a reference to him as the pillar of the bank was also to be deleted. Instead, Seth Shanti Prasad Jain was to be given at least two pages as a maker of modern India. Further, the gentlemen he had nominated on the board were to be given prominent importance, particularly, Seth Sheetal Prasad Jain, who was to be described as the 'Wizard of Indian Finance'. I tried to accommodate some points but could not fully endorse the approach of Seth Shanti Prasad Jain. When the history of

PNB, which I had laboriously compiled after over one-and-half years of research and scores of interviews with those who worked and laboured for it in the pre-partition era, was ready in its printed pre-order format, Seth Shanti Prasad Jain stopped it from being printed and released, even though he had earlier written a foreword for it. A larger than life mention about him was included in the final version approved by him including his full-page photograph.

On or about 19 December 1955, Seth Shanti Prasad Jain called me and wanted me to propose to the Board of Directors that his photograph be displayed at every branch of the bank. I have never been able to fathom the reason for him asking me to have his photographs put up at a prominent place in every branch of the bank. I discussed the matter with the General Manager and other senior colleagues who were equally amazed that Seth Shanti Prasad Jain did not seem inclined to adopt the policy of remaining out of public eye, until the public forgot episodes concerning the Dalmia Jain Group. I made it clear to Jain after consulting my senior colleagues that this was not the appropriate time to have his photograph installed in all the branches of the bank. The bombshell was to follow later.

There was a meeting of the Board of Directors on 28 December 1955, at Calcutta. There was a healthy tradition established a long time ago that all loan proposals beyond the limit of Rs. 5 lakhs, which were not approved by any authority in the bank, were put up in a summary form to the Directors recording the reasons for rejections, and, as a matter of routine, the Board made a note of these rejections.

The idea behind this practice was that the management of the bank was always to follow a healthy practice, where nobody dealing with the bank was denied a facility due to any bias or malice but only on merit. Due to reasons of confidentiality, I cannot divulge the proceedings at this Board Meeting. Suffice it to say that during the proceedings at the meeting, certain controversial resolutions were passed by the Board, which were detrimental to the interests of the PNB and I was telephonically informed about these developments.

On the receipt of these phone calls, I rushed to the bank and based on the duplicate set of agenda papers of the board, I prepared a letter dated 29 December 1955, addressed to the Observer, T.A. Vasvani, Deputy Chief Officer, Department of Banking Operations, RBI at New Delhi, and delivered the same to him at his residence at about 8:30 a.m.

By around 9:30 a.m., I was told that the Governor Sir Benegal Rama Rau of the RBI in Bombay (1949-1957) had instructed the head of the Calcutta office of RBI that the Chairman S.P. Jain be formally informed that the entire proceedings of the Board of Directors held on 28 December 1955 were frozen and no part thereof was to be implemented.

Apparently, by passing the various resolutions on 28 December 1955, the Chairman had *de facto* acquired powers to manage the bank. This direction of the RBI must have caused him shock and a serious setback.

On the return of B.N. Puri and P.R. Mehta from Calcutta, the senior executives got together and prepared and sent a deed of pledge to the Chairman. The operative part of the deed of pledge signed by nine executives, including myself, dated 2 January 1956, was as follows:

> "Being custodians of the savings of the nation, it is our duty to look to the safety of the bank's funds while considering all proposals of loans, investment of funds and schemes of expenditure. We will consider only those proposals which arise in due course according to the bank's set procedure, and will not subscribe our agreement to any financial transaction, which we do not conscientiously believe to be in the best interests of the bank's depositors. We shall not let temptations of personal reward or fear of punishment influence our judgment."

The pledge also said that "without any pressure of any kind we have affixed our signature hereto for the purpose of unreservedly subscribing thereto and solemnly promising to live up to them even at the pain of dismissal from service."

In the meantime, B.N. Puri had met the Finance Minister, C.D. Deshmukh, and told him of the crisis that Seth Shanti Prasad Jain was creating in the bank. Deshmukh mentioned that PNB was prone to runs and the management should be extra cautious to maintain high liquidity, while the Government on its part would continue to take steps to contain any adverse circumstances that might devolve on the bank. Deshmukh suggested that Puri should keep in touch with him in writing so that all developments were properly recorded and the bank was not exposed to any unnecessary risks. After his meeting with the Finance Minister, Puri called in all the senior executives to apprise them of his discussions with the Finance Minister and he recorded an official note of what had transpired between him and the Finance Minister.

The Chairman, Jain asked to be provided with an independent room in keeping with his status at the head office at Delhi. A day earlier T.A. Vasvani had called on B.N. Puri, General Manager, PNB, to finalise his seating arrangement as an Observer of the bank as appointed by the Reserve Bank of India. After mutual consultations in the core executive group, it was agreed that the room next to the General Manager, occupied by the Secretary to the Board be allotted to Vaswani and another room at the right angle to it, be refurbished and placed at the exclusive disposal of the chairman. For the coming three months that I continued attending the office, the Chairman Seth Shanti Prasad Jain availed of the facility of the room only once for a few hours. T.A. Vasvani, Observer, PNB, occupied the room immediately after it was offered and regularly attended the office.

In between the conclusion of the December Board Meeting of PNB and somewhere in the first week of January 1956, the Chairman informed B.N. Puri, the General Manager, that he had received complaints of serious financial irregularities in the functioning of the Public Relations Department headed by me ever since it was established in 1949 and he had instructed that the department be audited by the bank's statutory auditors. As usual, the matter was placed before the Core Group. I told the Group that I wanted to come out clean. Thus, the special audit, as the Chairman wanted to be put in place, commenced immediately. I decided to fully cooperate with this special audit.

After five weeks or so, General Manager Puri called me to say that the findings of the statutory auditors had been forwarded by the Chairman to him for further action. The General Manager read out relevant portions:

1. A spending department, involving public relations and economic research, had no authority to incur any daily expenditure of miscellaneous type except what the PRO was entitled to, from his budget proposals placed before and duly approved by the Board. There were exceptional circumstances which the PRO had not foreseen and where he had regularly approached the secretary and now GM (B.N. Puri) for necessary approval. In one case involving expenditure, where D.V.T. having no designation at that time had incurred expenses as his cab charges. The expenditure at Delhi in this case was submitted to the Secretary Board (Amarnath Chopra) for approval.

2. All the expenses were paid out, where required, in cash, but mostly through cheques after the perusal of Secretary, (later GM) had examined them and finally approved by the Superintendent, Central Accounts.

3. The auditors reported that their major job content was in paying specific and special attention to the expenses incurred in connection with the Diamond Jubilee celebrations of PNB in 1955. The auditors recorded that there were very few instances of cash disbursement. All other payments were made through cheques in accordance with

budget amounts approved by the Board. There was good scrutiny by the accounts department before making any payment.

4. There was no major irregularity worth reporting as a result of this special audit.

As desired by the Chairman, a copy of the report was given to me for my comments.

I said I had no comments to offer, as it was a factual report.

When the papers were put up to the Chairman, he ordered:

(i) The Public Relations Department including the Economic Adviser's functions be dissolved. Assistant Secretary (staff) A.S. Puri may transfer staff so spared at appropriate places.

(ii) D.V. Taneja be transferred as Manager, Nagpur branch.

Before the first week of April 1956, when the orders were received as expected, I had proceeded on three months' privilege leave due to me. This was the last time I served PNB when I vacated my room and said goodbye to my colleagues.

After I proceeded on leave, in my absence, I learnt that events had transpired in the following manner.

Executives had started approaching the Observer for his views and by-passing the General Manager i.e., B.N. Puri.

(iii) The Board Meeting in the presence of the Observer became a non-event, as the Observer had given 'in principle' approval to the agenda papers.

5. First B.N. Puri, and then P.R. Mehta, the Assistant Secretary (Loans) proceeded on leave. R.L.Tuli, Assistant Secretary, (Head Office) replaced B.N. Puri in his absence.

6. There was a simultaneous period affecting the three of us, when we three were together on leave. At that time we started meeting at B.N. Puri's residence. (The event that took place, i.e., the 'Mundhra lunch' has been separately dealt with). Puri was assured of a job at the expiry of his leave in the Central Bank of India.

I decided not to appeal to the Chairman regarding my transfer to Nagpur because mine was the first case relating to his acquisition of staff powers. It was felt that he was not likely to re-think over the matter.

Having suffered a severe setback due to freezing of the decisions of the Board Meeting held on 28 December 1955, and appointment of an Observer, Seth Shanti Prasad Jain retaliated on 8 February 1956.

There were clashes in the Board of PNB in the meeting of 8 February 1956. One director voted against the resolution that all powers relating to personnel matters would vest in the Board. All the nine signatories who took the pledge on 2 January 1956, made a joint representation on 10 February 1956, stating how such an order would disrupt the working of the bank. A copy of the representation was sent to C.D. Deshmukh, the Finance Minister. It was brought to the notice of the Honourable Minister that this would create a wrong impression on the minds of the staff and reduced the status of the General Manager to that of a dummy.

Pandit J.N. Bhan, Director, who was present in the Board Meeting, stated that certain points recorded in the minutes were never raised in the Board Meeting.

C.D. Deshmukh confirmed to B.N. Puri that nobody in the bank working in the interest of the bank would be allowed to be harmed. This statement carried an impression that Deshmukh was seriously considering nationalizing the PNB. Such decisions were seldom recorded in office files due to fear of serious repercussions in the stock market.

In the meantime, C.D. Deshmukh resigned in July 1956, and T.T. Krishnamachari was reported to be the next Finance Minister. The four of us—B.N. Puri, P.R. Mehta, myself and N.K. Mehta, (who controlled Bombay division)—had constantly been in touch with the RBI to apprise the RBI of all such developments, which T.A. Vasvani might not have been able to report to it. As soon as Deshmukh resigned, the four of us, who were in the forefront in resisting Jain's decisions, felt that there did not appear to be any option except to put in our resignations. The other five signatories on the pledge had their domestic responsibilities and even though R.L. Tuli, who had been instrumental in the preparation of pledge, started wavering, Seth Shanti Prasad Jain kept various other executives under pressure.

The Government appointed two bodies to investigate further into the workings of the Dalmia-Jain Group of companies. The first Commission of Enquiry on the administration of Dalmia-Jain companies was appointed on 11 December 1956, under the chairmanship of Justice S.R. Tendulkar. Another commission of enquiry, entitled the

Justice Vivian Bose Commission, examined the broad parameters of the manner in which the Dalmia-Jain group operated. Prime Minister Jawaharlal Nehru stated in his address to the Federation of the Indian Chambers of Commerce and Industry (FICCI) that it had caused him great anguish over the way business had been portrayed and conducted, as disclosed by the report of Justice Vivian Bose Commission.

15

New Innings at the Central Bank of India and Meeting Pandit Nehru

Before submitting our formal resignations, I decided to call on the Prime Minister, Pandit Jawaharlal Nehru, at his residence with a prior appointment. I went to meet him along with P.R. Mehta, Assistant Secretary, Loans Division, Head Office. However, I decided to initiate the discussion with the Prime Minister, as I had earlier met him on some other matters and believed that the nodding acquaintance might be of some help. This meeting with the Prime Minister, which occurred a week or so before the Board Meeting on 23 July 1956, started on an angry note by the Prime Minister and ended with a stormy parting. He did not allow me to complete my first sentence and instead, started reprimanding me. The main emphasis of his reproach was that the Government fully understood its responsibilities. He also emphasized that the PNB was safe in the hands of Seth Shanti Prasad Jain and that we were wrong in opposing him. When I politely interjected that the bank could sink under Seth Shanti Prasad Jain's leadership, the Prime Minster retorted and asked me where it would sink. I told him politely and respectfully that it would sink into the sea. At this stage, he was even more annoyed. The contents of his subsequent observations could not be fully comprehended but he appeared to be suggesting that the chairman in a public corporate body was the ultimate repository of trust and his orders had to be carried out. He was perhaps confused in his thinking about the difference between a Chairman nominated on the Board of Directors, and the Executive Chairman of the bank. As our talks were not making headway and the Prime Minister looked very upset, Mehta and I got up and thanked him for sparing his time. He shook hands with us and walked a little way to see us off.

Gulzarilal Nanda Asks for Our Resignations

B.N. Puri and Gulzarilal Nanda, Minister in the Central Cabinet, hailed from the same village—Ghartal District, Gujarat in Western Punjab (now in Pakistan). They were close to each other. Puri had kept Nanda apprised of the developments in the bank. Nanda had been sympathetic to our cause and used to mention that the Cabinet supported our stand. It was a strange coincidence that the same afternoon, after our meeting with the Prime Minister, B.N. Puri received a phone call from Gulzarilal Nanda asking Puri to meet him immediately. Gulzarilal Nanda told Puri that we had lost the support of the Cabinet and that we should resign. After the meeting with Gulzarilal Nanda, the four of us, out of the nine signatories to the pledge, submitted our resignations, thus severing our association with the PNB.

Seth Shanti Prasad Jain did not give a chance to the remaining signatories to the pledge, who stayed behind, to manage the bank. He recruited three British executives from

England to run the PNB, when in fact it was the PNB which was the first *Swadeshi* bank started in 1895, when India was trying to free itself from foreign rule. This was a great irony in the scheme of things that independent India had no suitable Indian to manage this *Swadeshi* institution. T.A. Walker, the British General Manager, once sent for me asking me to clarify my observations in one of the files. This was the only time when I met Walker.

Haridas Mundhra

Somewhere during the end of June or early July 1956, I received an unusual request, which concerned one Haridas Mundhra. As per the request, Mundhra wanted me to arrange a meeting between himself and the executives who had ceased attending the bank or had resigned. I gathered the background of Mundhra. My colleagues and I had heard about him that he had suddenly appeared on the business scene and was acquiring a large number of British managed firms. Those who were in contact with him said that he appeared aggressive and a man in a great hurry. After consulting my colleagues, B.N. Puri and P.R. Mehta, it was decided to invite him for lunch, concerning which Mundhra mentioned that there were certain pre-conditions. His requirements were that a Brahmin should cook his food, the water that he would use must come from a well, and, also, he gave me a list of vegetables which he ate. After the lunch was over, he explained to us that his ambitions were unlimited and boasted that all the government agencies and departments, including ministers, danced to his tunes and he could get anything done and that his influence was overwhelming. He offered B.N. Puri a salary of Rs. 15,000 per month and P.R. Mehta, Rs. 10,000 per month if they would join him to take over the charge of his group's organizations and finances. We informed Mundhra that Messrs Puri and Mehta had not yet left the bank officially and could make no commitments at this stage. Further, we wanted to know more about him and his organizations to which he replied that he would send us all the information (which we never received). He spent over three hours with the three of us, that is, Messrs Puri, Mehta and myself. We did not hear from him ever again.

In the winter session of the Parliament in 1957, there was a major controversy involving the stock market, Haridas Mundhra and the Life Insurance Corporation of India (LIC). This controversy was hotly debated in Parliament. Due to the matter being highly sensitive in nature, T.T. Krishnamachari, the Finance Minister was left with no option except to pay heed, in view of the agitated and hostile reaction in Parliament, to the most irresponsible manner in which Mundhra's transactions were put through with the LIC. The Government had, therefore, to appoint a Commission of Enquiry on 17 January 1958, to be headed by Justice M.C. Chagla, the Chief Justice of Bombay High Court, to investigate the LIC-Mundhra deal and report its findings.

Justice Chagla's Commission held the investments by the LIC in the Mundhra concerns to be irregular and improper. He further held that while the constitutional responsibility for the deal rested with the Finance Minister, H.M. Patel, who was the Principal Finance Secretary had played a leading role in arranging the transactions. He also rejected the plea of the Principal Finance Secretary, i.e. H.M. Patel that LIC had invested the money to overcome a crisis in the Calcutta Stock Exchange. Accepting constitutional responsibility, T.T. Krishnamachari resigned from the Cabinet.

The debate in Parliament and the anger that raged as a result, led the Prime Minister to constitute another enquiry board comprising Justice Vivian Bose of the Supreme Court of India, who was to head the investigation as its Chairman. S. Sen, the Chief Election Commissioner, and Satyanathan, Chief Secretary to the Government of Madras, were nominated to act as members of the Board. There were differences in the conclusions of Justice Vivian Bose's enquiry board and the Union Public Service Commission (UPSC) about what should be done regarding H.M. Patel. Justice Bose's board recommended that Patel should be compulsorily retired. UPSC wanted Patel to be exonerated. However, the Government ultimately decided that no action would be taken against H M Patel.

Lessons Learnt from PNB

In July 1956, when I left the PNB, I was 32 years old and had 12 years of banking experience. The most important lesson that I learnt was from the aftermath of events in Pakistan, which resulted in unsettled social and economic conditions. Under the leadership of the seniors in the bank, I might have made a small contribution towards the success of their efforts. However, when the Dalmia-Jain Group threw a challenge and started adopting tactics, which were against principles of ethics, truth and transparency, as the youngest in the team of bankers in PNB, I defended the institution, i.e., the PNB, based on the premise that a banker is a trustee of depositors and I had to fight for the cause of PNB.

During the period of July to October 1956, I started working in a friend's office as a clerk writing accounts at the rate of Rs. 8 per hour.

Joining the Federation of Indian Chambers of Commerce and Industry

An unusual and surprising development took place when I received a call from Seth Shanti Prasad Jain in the last week of October 1956. He wanted me to have breakfast with him. During the course of our one-to-one conversation, he said that he did not want me to resign from my job at PNB, but in the heat of the moment, he had included my name in the list of people whom he wanted to leave. He felt that I should find a suitable job and carve out a proper career for myself. In the meantime, he had arranged that I should join the Federation of Indian Chambers of Commerce and Industry. He telephoned G.L. Bansal, Secretary General of FICCI, to find out if he was in the office. I took him in my car to the office of FICCI. On his inquiry about my using an old model car, I told him that my friends among the staff of PNB had raised some funds by voluntary contributions to enable me to have a conveyance after I surrendered the office car to PNB.

After introducing me to G.L. Bansal, it was decided that I would work as an assistant to the Secretary General and would start working immediately.

CENTRAL BANK OF INDIA

Immediately after leaving the PNB, B.N. Puri joined The Central Bank of India Limited as Controller of the Northern Group of offices with headquarters in Delhi on 1 August, 1956. On 30 November, 1956 B.N. Puri telephoned me and conveyed to me the news that he had the approval from the head office of the Central Bank of India saying that I could join Central Bank. He insisted that I must report for duty on the same day. I explained the situation to Bansal of FICCI and told him that in lieu of notice, he may forfeit my salary for the month of November 1956. I also thanked Seth S.P. Jain for his kind thought, courtesy and consideration. By this gracious gesture, Jain restored our mutual relationship to one of understanding and respect. (When I shifted to Bombay in 1965 and started living there on a permanent basis, I had the pleasure of having meals with both Seth S.P. Jain and Seth Shriyans Prasad Jain on a few occasions at their invitation.)

However, the delay that took place initially in my appointment at the Central Bank of India was due to strong opposition from the executives serving at the headquarters of the Central Bank of India in Bombay. I think a formula was evolved that the emoluments offered to me by the Central Bank of India would be two-thirds of what I was getting from PNB, where a number of allowances had been devised to give me a comfortable take-home package, even though my basic salary was low. It was thought by the executives at Bombay that I might not accept a one-third cut in my take-home salary and would refuse to join, particularly, when I had a regular job and I had started working in FICCI. However, the *raison d'etre* in my joining the Central Bank of India was that I did not want to be discourteous to Puri, who had blessed me with a great deal of affection and protection in PNB. I was also keen to have a career in banking and I thought that a similar opportunity might never present itself again.

16
A Stint with Literature: 1946 Onwards and India's Leaders Post-independence

In the middle of 1946, while working in PNB at Lahore, I found that the pressure of work in the bank had suddenly dwindled. There were expectations all over the country that India would soon attain freedom. The British were not taking any initiatives on policy matters of economic dimensions. There were no new enterprises being established. Banks had equally become cautious in making fresh commitments. In the changed circumstances on normal days, I would finish my work within an hour or so. Slowly, it dawned on me that I should continue writing short stories in Hindi. During this period until the end of the 1950s, I wrote some short stories. Whenever my father had time, he would reproduce my stories in his handwriting, which was firm and better than mine.

At the same time, I started composing poems in English. During my college days, my Professor of English Literature evoked my interest in the lives and writings of English poets.

Between 1946 and until I got transferred to Bombay in 1964, I composed a large number of poems, some of which ran into more than 25 printed pages. Between 1958 and 1963, I also wrote a book on the principles of economics and a volume on human resource development, which are yet to be published.

Reflections in a Mirror: My First Publication

Writing poems in English became an obsession with me. I published my first volume called *Reflections in a Mirror* in New Delhi in January 1963. This book comprised 51 poems running into 180 pages. I was convinced at that time that I had the necessary equipment and strength to enter the literary world. In my Preface to the book, I stated: "My mind would overflow and I could only get peace after I had recorded my reactions." I chose 51 of the poems written up to 1961 and I wanted some eminent person from the literary world to write a foreword for me.

Dr. S. Radhakrishnan, Vice-President and President of India (1888-1975)

I got in touch with Dr S. Radhakrishnan in June 1961 who was then Vice President of India and an eminent scholar. I left with him a copy of the typed manuscript of my book of poems and proposed that he may consider writing a foreword.

Dr Radhakrishnan advised me that he would go through my manuscript but he might not be able to write any foreword. In his letter dated 6 July 1961, sent to me, which is reproduced in *Reflections in a Mirror,* he also stated: "Your enthusiasm and linguistic equipment are impressive. I do not think the book requires any foreword."

When Dr Radhakrishnan was elected President, I sought another appointment with him. He signed the book on the blank page *'Best wishes, S. Radhakrishnan, 18/08/63'.* In that meeting with the President I told him, in reply to his question, that I was the son of a Sanskrit scholar whom everybody called *Panditji*, though we were not Brahmins. He immediately started reciting *Kritis* in Sanskrit for about 15 minutes. As soon as he finished his recitation, I rose from the seat where I was sitting. Dr Radhakrishnan had received me in his bedroom and was reclining in his bed. He extended his hand, which I warmly shook. I thanked him for all the courtesies and took his leave.

Dr Zakir Hussain, the Vice President of India (1897-1969)

Reverting to the book *Reflections in a Mirror*, I decided to call on the then Vice President Dr Zakir Hussain on 22 August, 1963. Dr Zakir Hussain was a great man with disarming humility and courtesies. Before deciding to meet him, I felt I should try to converse with him in Urdu of which the Vice President was a great scholar.

Initially, after the customary greetings between us, he immediately reverted to speaking in English, perhaps due to the fact that the book, which I had earlier sent to him was in English and he thought that I would be more comfortable in the English language.

Apart from some initial observations, Dr Zakir Hussain continued to engage in pleasant conversation, which focused on what I had written in the book. He had laid a feast of eatables on a table in the corner of his rose garden. We sat in a relaxed atmosphere for more than half an hour. He autographed the book as requested by me.

Other dignitaries

Another two dignitaries to autograph the book were Vijaya Lakshmi Pandit and Chester Bowles, who was then the Ambassador of US to India. The book had a receptive press. There were about a dozen reviews of the book.

Each of the aforesaid personalities had an enormous impact on me during my early days in banking and in my stint with literature.

My book of poems, *Reflections in a Mirror,* has now been published in the United States of America. This is a great honour for me and I consider it a privilege that this initial publication of 1963 has now, after 50 years, been considered worthy of publication, in the United States of America.

Extracts from book reviews published in 1963 in different Indian newspapers/magazines concerning my book of poems are given below:

"The verse comes straight from the heart. It is emotion crystalised directly into word and music, as if the flesh stood aside so that the spirit may pour forth...

Among the poems there are little pretty pieces as well as long poems. Some of the longer poems show the poet at his best. For flight of imagination, intellectual sweep and philosophic content, as least two of them are masterpieces."

– The Sunday Standard

"There is in these 'poems' a kind of sincerity, a tolerance, gentleness and an overriding good temper with life and humanity."

– The Hindustan Times

"A rich and entertaining fare to suit all moods and all literary palates. A book of verse to buy, to read, to keep."

– *Blitz*

"It is a 'must' for all college and public libraries so that discriminating readers are in a position to know for themselves the contribution which writers like Mr. Taneja have made to the enrichment of Indo-Anglian literature."

– *The Tribune*

"These reflections indicate a poet wrapt in meditation, contemplating from the brink of time to the river of life as it flows past slavery, freedom, truth, woman and the 'young ascetic', who is described as 'not a man'. In his freedom from the restraint of rhyme or metre he approaches the skill of Walt Whitman. Like him too he is moved by noble thoughts and again like him the thoughts pour out in a cascade that is not easily checked and is always of the utmost sincerity."

– *The Hindu*

"If the quality of these early efforts is so excellent, it will be difficult to imagine what the quality of his subsequent efforts will be. One has to see them in print in order to believe them."

– *Indian Foreign Affairs*

"Energy and sentiments are his strong points and his chief merit."

– *The National Herald*

"Mr. Taneja has a robust philosophy and devout optimism. His ideas crystallize into exquisite cadences.... He lapses himself in Lydian airs through glorious verses."

– *Amrita Bazar Patrika*

"A collection of 51 poems "Reflections In A Mirror" runs the whole gamut from ecstatic lyricism to moods of autumnal sorrow. It is not a casual miscellany, but an integrated ensemble of poetic insights, expressed not in terms of verbal gloss, but of profound and sincere feeling. Like that great American poet, the late Wallace Stevens, Mr. Taneja is a business executive who has not allowed his sensibilities to be blunted by the humdrum of corporate existence. In his own way, he demonstrates the power of the Muse to prevail over the deadening anodyne of mere routine.

– *Deccan Herald*

"The skill and cunning with which the poet converts even a seemingly prosaic subject into fine poetry are commendable....

There is a strength and sanity about Mr. Taneja's approach to the larger issues of life which can prove to be diet and medicine for morbid minds.... All in all *Reflections in a Mirror* is a significant contribution to Indo-Anglian verse."

– *Mainstream*

"Taneja's verse has a force and flow and freedom which stamp it as something distinct and distinguished. The phrases and lines and stanzas follow one after the other in such abundance and with such abandon that the reader has the experience of confronting a veritable river of poetry. There is such passion and enthusiasm everywhere that truly there is nothing which can stop the 'songs of the poet's heart."

– *Citizen of India*

"Mr. Taneja's choice of English as the medium for his muse does not prevent his thought from ranging with grace and self-confidence over a wide horizon of experience...."

– *Link*

"*Reflections* offer varied, exciting fare. To the practical man there is much to enthuse him; to the philosophically inclined much to brood about; to the wise much to speak about; to the ignorant much to learn about."

– *Patriot*

"Anyone who goes through this book with attention will probably like it, and find himself profited."

– *The Mail*

"It is really a work of art on life the reflections of which are mirrored in it."

– *Search Light*

I have never formally learnt Sanskrit, except of course having read the *Bhagvad Gita* in Sanskrit with its English translation, several times during various stages and decades of my life. I was also inspired by the expositions given by my father of the *Bhagvad Gita*. My father used to visit various prominent personalities of undivided Punjab and subsequently at Delhi, where he was engaged especially to provide interpretations of the philosophy of the *Bhagvad Gita* in English, which was the language the members of his audience were most comfortable with. My father first recited the original Sanskrit text and thereafter he amplified literal and various intellectual and philosophical meanings given to each stanza. In college in Lahore, he used to teach Kalidas' *Shakuntalam* to his students of Sanskrit, as prescribed by the University of Lahore for their BA classes.

PANDIT JAWAHARLAL NEHRU, PRIME MINISTER OF INDIA (1889-1964)

When *Reflections in a Mirror* was published, I wrote to the Prime Minister that I wanted to present my book to him and I asked him whether he would accept my dedication to him. Prompt came the reply, signed by him that he would gladly see me and accept the dedication. I met him on the morning of 25 September 1963, and he signed a copy for me. The Ministry of Information photographed the event and the pictures were printed in several newspapers the next day. I had also asked for an appointment with Mrs. Indira Gandhi. She signed on the same date on the opening blank page.

PANDIT NEHRU: SAPRU HOUSE, NEW DELHI

It was always a pleasure and a privilege to be asked to be of some assistance to the Prime Minister. My first meeting with Panditji took place when he appeared to have spoken to Lala Yodhraj in 1950, saying that he wanted the Punjab National

Bank Ltd to be bankers to receive donations for Sapru House, which was to be built on Barakhamba Road, New Delhi, in the memory of Sir Tej Bahadur Sapru. As PNB was going to be the banker, he wanted the bank to prepare an appeal for donations. He would sign the appeal and asked this to be organized. I was as at that time the PRO of the bank. Lala Yodhraj asked me to undertake this responsibility.

My own knowledge of Sir Tej Bahadur Sapru (1875-1949) was rather sketchy at the time. My father, to whom I turned for help, too had a very limited idea about his background. From what I could gather from the research that I briefly did at the time, Sir Sapru had played an effective role in 1928 to draft a constitution for the future of independent India, apart from his constructive participation at the Round Table Conference in London. He was nominated as a delegate to the Constituent Assembly, during which he had helped in preparing the chapter on Fundamental Rights in the Indian Constitution.

I drafted the appeal emphasizing some of the aforesaid points and I took it personally to the Prime Minister. Before I could say anything, he signed the appeal and told me to remember that Rs. 3,50,000 was the estimated cost and he expected the bank to raise the necessary amount.

Panditji also told me that PNB and its associates were required to donate a at least Rs. 50,000 and asked me to keep his office informed about the progress in collection of donations. While I rose to leave, Panditji made a passing reference that the foundation of India's future would rest on a proper interpretation and implementation of the Constitution. He mentioned that he would pass on the supervision and control of the building at Sapru House, whenever it was ready, to the Supreme Court of India for research and help to prepare future constitutional experts.

The appropriate funds were raised. The building was declared open in 1955. In 2005, when I visited Sapru House to refresh my memory about the people who had made donations from the marble plaque on which the list is inscribed, to my surprise, I found that the offices of the Indian Council of World Affairs are located there and its excellent auditorium had been shut down for some years.

Pandit Nehru: Conceptualizing the Ashok Hotel, New Delhi

Pandit Nehru conceived the idea of having a world class hotel representing, at the same time, the classical characteristics of Hindu and Muslim architecture. The hotel was going to cost a sizeable sum of money, a small portion of which a local entrepreneur was prepared to subscribe. By the time the project report was ready, Panditji asked his staff to contact me to find out whether the Central Bank of India, which was the largest private sector bank at that time, would be prepared to finance the project. Once we got the 'in principle' approval of the proposal from our head office in Bombay, the project was announced and Panditji decided that it would be called the Ashok Hotel. One of the conditions of the bank's approval was that it would have the exclusive right to have a branch in the premises of the hotel, to which the authorities agreed. (A branch of the Central Bank has, since 1959 or so, continued to function from the Ashok Hotel through a fully service-oriented office and a round-the-clock outlet to serve the guests of the Ashok Hotel).

The operational side of financing the project was transferred to one of the senior managers (then called agents) of Central Bank's principal branch in New Delhi. Without taking the head office in Bombay or the controlling office in Delhi into confidence, the manager concerned had one day got a huge sign board in black wooden lettering drilled into the stone façade, covering the whole of the wall of the Ashok Hotel, taking care at the same time that the glass windows of the bank came right below the inscribed name. It looked as if it was not a hotel, but that the building belonged to the Central Bank itself!

I did not know about this development until I received a telephone from the agent (manager) of the Central Bank branch at Ashok Hotel, saying that the Prime Minister wanted me forthwith to have the huge lettering dismantled immediately and he was very upset at the bank having put its own inscription, covering the entire building.

Within hours, I had the lettering removed. Fortunately for me, Panditji was busy in a meeting during the period when I had the lettering removed. Nevertheless, the confirmation of the inscription having been removed was conveyed to Pandit Nehru.

Pandit Jawaharlal Nehru will rank after Gandhiji as the builder of modern India in having laid down the foundation of a functioning democracy.

17

My Association with Central Bank of India

In terms of Indian banking, and my role as an Indian banker, I consider the time spent in Central Bank of India as the most pivotal and significant period in my career. I would divide my association of 19 years with The Central Bank of India Ltd., which was later nationalized and known as Central Bank of India, under the following heads:

1. **Delhi (1956 to 1964): Tasks Undertaken**

(a) I assisted in opening as many branches of Central Bank of India as existed during the aforesaid period in India of Punjab National Bank, keeping in view the fact that most of these branches were in residential areas with high potential of deposits. I tried to ensure that the service offered to the public was quick and better than the position prevailing at the relevant time in other banks.

(b) The majority union in Delhi was affiliated to Indian National Trade Union Congress (INTUC) and was more aggressive than the local minority union, holding affiliation to the Communist Party. The abrasive character of the majority union was slowly, but firmly, brought within discipline, respect for work and devotion to duty.

(c) In the meantime, it appeared that pressure was building up by the Chairman, Sir Homi Modi and Vice-Chairman, C.H. Bhabha who, because of their visits to Delhi and interaction with me, had suggested to the management to transfer me to Bombay despite opposition from the executive cadre at the head office. For instance, in 1961 I was posted at the head office for about three months where I was to assist in preparation of Golden Jubilee celebrations of the bank, a role similar to the one which I had played in organizing the Diamond Jubilee celebrations of PNB in 1955. I could feel the tension that my presence was creating at that time at the head office in Bombay. The MD and CEO, N.K. Karanjia retired in 1963. He had rendered credible and illustrious banking service for several decades and had also spent a decade as CEO. He was succeeded by F.C. Cooper, General Manager and CEO, who was also a chartered accountant and a professional banker. During a visit to Delhi around 1964, Cooper had long sessions and discussions with me, paving the ground for my transfer to Bombay, simultaneously, with the retirement of B.N. Puri in July 1964 as Controller of Northern Group of officers in Delhi. This turn of events took place in the wider context, when jokingly I used to ask the Chairman, Vice-Chairman, Managing Director and successor General Manager whether any of them had ever visited all the 30 chief agents who controlled a small cluster of offices and enjoyed wide powers or whether they knew or had seen all of them collectively or individually except those in Calcutta, Delhi, Madras and a couple of other major cities. At the insistence of F.C. Cooper, I prepared an exhaustive note for holding the first ever Chief Agents' conference in Bombay. Once the approach paper was accepted, I was asked to report at Bombay to see through the preparation and conclusions of the conference. I stayed in Bombay for six months and the various executives formed their own impressions about me. I was permanently posted in Bombay after the conclusion of the conference to follow up planning and development of the bank on certain well-laid outlines of action.

2. Bombay: Early 1965 to My Termination in 1975

Change in strategic policies of Central Bank of India

The strategy I evolved in consultation with the committee of senior executives from 1965 onwards was that different problems that the bank was facing at that time should be dealt with, as far as possible, simultaneously. The policy of concentration of power in one person and a bureaucratized style of functioning was turning out to be an impediment in changes of policy to accelerate the progress of the bank. After reaching a consensus and with the approval of the management, I embarked on a very fast expansion of branches with the existing staff, through internal promotions, as that would cast away the element of frustration that was at that time making forward movement difficult.

To create a psychological impact on the market, after initial preparations and licenses from the RBI the bank opened 51 branches in one day with backup publicity.

Taking charge of Personnel Department of Central Bank of India

At the same time, I initiated discussions with the union leaders to ascertain what their problems were. For any trivial issue, the entire bank staff, comprising about 2000 people at the head office, would take out metal plates and start beating them with wooden sticks and created a din, at the same time giving a call to the staff to stop working. This practice had to stop. I told them that before they undertook this method of creating all these noises, they should bring to my notice the precise nature of their problems.

Simultaneously, the branches through their Chief Agents had been persuaded to prepare their plans and budgets and these were put to quarterly review.

At this stage, the Board of Directors realized that if I could devote my entire time to handling personnel matters that could relieve the top management, both at the Chief Agents' level and Head Office level, of the constant disruption which over a period of recent months had become less of a nuisance.

As a consequence, I was given overall charge of the Personnel Department. In the meantime, more Chief Agents' conferences were held with different conveners and this led to better interaction between the head office and its branches. This helped the bank to accelerate its growth and earn better profitability.

RECOGNITION OF ALL INDIA CENTRAL BANK EMPLOYEES' FEDERATION AS THE SOLE BARGAINING AGENT

In 1967, it became apparent that the staff had become disinterested over a period of time in the working of the bank, having no motivation, and, in most cases, the staff colluded with their agents in medium and small branches in having developed a mutual understanding of aimless disinterest.

It was also unfortunate that the Chief Agents, under whose direct control all the branches of the bank fell, adopted an easy-going approach about service to customers and the future of the bank. They had introduced 'contract overtime' based on the slogan—*O.T. Is Roti* (overtime provides food). I persuaded the senior management that the only solution that I could think of was that we should recognize the majority union, binding it to a code of conduct, make it the sole bargaining agent and after that enforce discipline, attendance and dedicated work to the extent we could get the cooperation of the staff. From my survey of how many entries in the books of accounts on an average a clerk made in a day, I found that from Amritsar to Calcutta the average came to 40 to 60; in Central India and in Maharashtra, it was better by 20 points; but, practically, in the whole of the south, the average entries made in the books of accounts per day came to 150/200. This was another eye opener and reflected the easy-going policy that agents and Chief Agents in most parts of the country followed, giving contractual overtime to buy local peace. Stating this in another context, if everyone were to put in the amount of work on the same scale that people in South India did, it would mean that a lot of staff was surplus.

On 30 April 1969, the bank recognized the All India Central Bank Employees' Federation (AICBEF), which was Communist affiliated, as the representative body of our bank's clerical and subordinate staff and the sole bargaining agent on behalf of the aforesaid category staff. Issues of an all-India nature would be negotiated and settled through this majority union. Debit authorities for payment of subscription towards membership of the respective union would constitute the basis to determine the majority and minority character of the concerned union on the local, regional and all-India level. Recognition was given to local unions where they owed allegiance to the rival group. The basic principle governing the relationship was that the management and unions agreed that no unilateral action or any industrial action would be undertaken by either party and all matters would be resolved through discussions at the appropriate level. Further, the unions agreed, among other things, not to engage in any form of physical duress; the union members would not engage themselves during working hours in any other activity, other than performance of their duties as employees of the bank. The overall effect of the circular was that the staff, to the extent possible, engaged themselves in due performance of their duties. The other nationalized banks were not happy with Central Bank having signed an agreement with the majority union and in having brought about peace in India's largest nationalized bank.

In the last week of April, 1970, V.C. Patel, who was then the Custodian of the bank, called me and handed me a file detailing a report of Noshir M. Mistry from London on the affairs of London branch. Next morning, I reported to him that a serious fraud of large magnitude had taken place. This required further investigation. I suggested that S.J. Dhanboora, the bank's Legal Adviser, be flown to London as the matter had serious legal implications. He insisted that I go to Delhi and meet P.N. Haksar, Principal Secretary to the Prime Minister at New Delhi who could arrange the issuance of my passport without any delay, and, thereafter, I would be required to proceed to London immediately.

CHANGES IN THE BANK'S TOP MANAGEMENT

Subsequent to the retirement of V.C. Patel, Custodian of the bank, on 30 June 1970 (F.C. Cooper had died in January 1966 and V.C. Patel had succeeded him), Ramanand Rao, who had earlier held the position of Managing Director of State Bank of India, joined the bank as Custodian on 1 July 1970. However, Rao could not adjust himself to the atmosphere of the Central Bank and resigned on 21 February 1971.

On the same date, B.N. Adarkar, who had earlier worked as Deputy Governor for five years and Governor of the RBI for 45 days, joined the bank as Custodian. Other senior executives—S.T. Parekh, T.N. Ramamurthy, B.R. Patel and Venkateshwar—had been retired in February 1970. P. Krishna Iyer joined the Bank on 2 June 1970, on deputation from RBI as an Officer on Special Duty, and left the bank on 31 March 1974.

FRAUD IN THE LONDON BRANCH OF CENTRAL BANK OF INDIA

I reached London, United Kingdom on 4 May 1970, and was immediately provided with the draft of an article, which had been prepared by the investigation team of *The Sunday Times* of London. They had been working on this case for almost a month and their draft mentioned different banks and versions of different parties involved in the case. I discussed the contents of this draft with N.M. Mistry and we decided that this one- sided version, which was biased against Central Bank, must be repudiated, for which purpose we jointly evolved a strategy. Apa B. Pant, the High Commissioner of India to the United Kingdom at the time, had in fact given me the draft prepared by *The Sunday Times* team and he had further told the daily that they should contact me so that I could provide them with the Central Bank's version.

In the meantime, the Bank of England sent for me after my arrival in London and I was received by a gentleman who presented himself as the Principal of the Bank of England. Without asking for any comments or explanation, he told me that if Central Bank of India did not meet its liabilities immediately, the Bank of England was considering to close down the Central Bank of India's branch in London. I pretended that this warning has had no effect on me, and in a very calm manner, I told him that this aspect was being considered by the authorities in India, and, in the event that the London branch of the Central Bank of India was directed or required to close down, the RBI would reciprocate by closing down all the British banks functioning in India. It appeared to me that he was not prepared for this reaction, and he suddenly changed his attitude. At this stage, I also mentioned to him that I had been deputed to London on the basis that Central Bank of India was a victim of fraud in conspiracy by British nationals, using the name of our bank to raise funds in Europe. The bank had decided to approach the police as well as file civil cases in the English courts to recover monies drawn fraudulently and through forgery by banks in Europe based on so-called guarantees of Central Bank of India. I added that Central Bank of India had complete faith in the English judicial system as well as the efficiency and integrity of the British Police. We would abide by any decision that the English courts took in due course. He changed his stance and said that we could depend on the support of the Bank of England.

I conveyed the gist of this conversation to the head office of Central Bank of India in Bombay, who apparently advised the RBI. Initially, they thought I had exceeded my brief. At the same time, it was considered appropriate that a senior RBI dignitary, M. Narasimaham should visit England and restore good relations between the two banking supervising/regulatory authorities. The delegation came and met the officials of the Bank of England, and they also called on the relevant persons in Europe. I was informed that the concerned authorities were convinced about the *bona fides* of Central Bank of India.

Following my long interviews on Saturday, 16 May 1970, at *The Sunday Times* headquarters, lasting about three hours, *The Sunday Times* published a balanced story in their London edition on 17 May 1970. They were frequently changing a cigar box lying in the centre of the table, which I thought was a voice-recording machine, because my oral statements were correctly stated and reproduced in an eight-column story with bold front page headlines. They wanted to print my photograph and I persuaded them that there could be serious security considerations to my life as well as the lives of others in the bank's team, and that they should not publish my photograph. The characters involved in the fraud were criminals. I needed the media's cooperation and *The Sunday Times'* protection.

When Sami Patel, the previous Manager of Central Bank of India, London branch, who had masterminded the fraud, was stabbed and found in a critical condition in Buenos Aires, *The Sunday Times* allowed me free use of their communication channels to send messages to our team and receive messages from our team there and this service was of great help to us. They maintained the highest ethics of journalism. They never printed a word about those messages in their paper. The *Daily Telegraph,* London, was also very helpful.

If I were to ascribe honours in the case to those who contributed to the successful conclusion of the matter, I would place it in the following order:

1. The Fraud Squad of the Metropolitan London Police, with whom I interacted for nearly three years: I pay tribute to their ingenuity, tact and speed with which they brought the case to a successful conclusion, leading to conviction of all the accused to 26 years' imprisonment, seven years maximum—the sentences were to run concurrently. Earlier, the jury unanimously held them guilty in one of the longest trials in British history.

2. Noshir M. Mistry, the chief investigation officer from the bank who alerted the head office about the fraud, was the star prosecution witness, who gave evidence for almost 45 days at a stretch. Unfortunately, he was made a victim by the London Police, who found forged currency notes which had been planted at his residence by the London Police itself, apparently at the instance of the accused, a couple of days before the start of the trial. The case against Mistry came to an ironic end when the same police officers, who claimed to have recovered the forged currency notes from his house, were themselves arrested by the customs authorities for

being in possession of banned drugs, forged Pounds Sterling and Dollar currency notes. It is to the credit of the Bank of England that they sent a formal letter through their solicitors withdrawing the case against Mistry. I appeared in the court at the final hearing, and in consultation with our counsel, Michael Sherrard, Queen's Counsel, the bank waived all claims of damages for defamation and mental torture suffered by Mistry and also in appreciation of the Metropolitan Police for their hard work in the main fraud case. It was the calmness, courage and boldness of Mistry that he continued to give evidence while the forgery case was hanging like a sword on his head. Later, after I left the bank, in due course, Mistry was appointed Chairman and Managing Director of the bank.

3. Vere Da Silva, the solicitor acting on behalf of the bank, and Senior Partner of Stocken & Co., Solicitors, London, worked incessantly in simplifying an extremely complicated case. He developed a line of thinking that this fraud was like running a bank fraudulently within a bank. This approach stood us in good measure in simplifying things.

On the civil side, scores of cases were filed against the London branch of Central Bank of India by the German banks, which had discounted bills drawn and accepted by paper companies and endorsed fraudulently by Sami Patel, supported in several cases with unauthorized and forged guarantees purportedly issued by Central Bank of India's London branch. The German banks realized that the case of Central Bank of India's London branch in the criminal proceedings, on the basis of which the accused were jailed, would weaken their case on the civil side.

S. Jagannathan, the Governor of the RBI telephoned me from Washington in early October 1972, saying that he was arriving in London on 7 October 1972, to see me and would stay with me. It appeared to me from the discussions we had that there had been certain diplomatic communications between the German Government and the Indian Government. Jagannathan told me that the Indian Cabinet had decided to settle the matter with the concerned banks on terms and conditions that the Central Bank officials in London, in consultations with solicitors and Senior Counsel, could negotiate. On his return to Bombay, RBI would be remitting sufficient funds to the credit of Central Bank's accounts with Bank of England. As soon as this matter was resolved in the first few months of 1973, all legal suits filed against each other were withdrawn. I left for India to report for duty as Deputy General Manager on 3 May 1973, in Bombay; this period of my career is described subsequently in this chapter.

Appointment of Senior Counsel from India

Initially, in May 1970, when I reached London and examined our evidence and had extensive discussions with Mistry, we decided to appoint Stocken & Co. as our Solicitors. I telephoned P.N. Haksar, Principal Secretary to the Prime Minister of India, Mrs Indira Gandhi, and informed him that the nature of the case was such that an eminent Senior Counsel from India should be appointed to visit us to guide us on an overall strategy to be adopted in this case. Niren De, the Attorney General of India, was deputed for the purpose.

After staying in London for a couple of days, he shifted to the house of his brother, Dr Dhiren De, who lived some 200 miles away from London, where our appointment was fixed to consult and meet Niren De. Our solicitors, B.D. Jayal, who was Minister Economic Affairs of the Indian High Commission, London, Mistry, myself and my wife making a total of eight persons, hired a special vehicle to reach there. Vere Da Silva and Niren De on one particular point differed in approach, but that issue was left to the decision of the bank. On the whole Niren De appeared to feel that our approach to the case was alright and he endorsed the steps taken so far. We travelled for about 16 hours both ways of the journey and had an audience with Niren De, which lasted for about half an hour. Reviewing our meeting with the Attorney General, Mistry and I came to the conclusion that we needed the advice and guidance of an eminent Senior Counsel from India who understood the commercial side of banking and business law. I again telephoned Haksar and asked him if he could get the permission of the Prime Minister to get Nani Palkhivala, who was the most distinguished Senior Counsel in India, so that he could be professionally engaged for this case, provided Palkhivala could occasionally spare some time to visit us in London. I explained to Haksar that in this manner, our head office in Bombay, we in London, and our solicitors in London could have the simultaneous benefit of his guidance. In the meantime, B.N. Adarkar brought with him K.T. Desai, former Chief Justice, Gujarat High Court, to London. Eventually, Nani Palkhivala was given the brief, and he was not only being consulted in Bombay by the management, but he also visited London a number of times.

He and our solicitors got on very well together and there was a smooth flow and interchange of information between Palkhivala and the solicitors. At the same time we had our say and we continued to be guided by him.

When on my return to India, a request was conveyed to Palkhivala to send to our solicitors his memorandum of fees, he took out the brief, wrote *gratis* on it and stated that he had undertaken this assignment as a service to the nation and he would not charge anything. This was the greatness of one of India's finest legal luminaries, and it was my honour to have known him.

Interaction with B.N. Adarkar

During my brief stay in India for consultations, I came into close contact with B.N. Adarkar, Custodian and later Chairman and Managing Director of the bank. I had to explain to him all the developments concerning the bank in London.

B.N. Adarkar was a great and meticulous gentleman. He was usually in the office by about 9 in the morning and left late in the evening, setting for us an example of punctuality. He was inclined to make long speeches, which were based on matters that did not require elaboration. He was trained in the art of writing detailed notes, amplifying his thoughts and appointing committees, but he was not trained in the art of running a bank, which required to be managed on a commercial basis where quick and on-the-spot decisions had to be made. I mentioned to him one day that as one holding the substantive post of Manager Personnel, I was planning to shift 150 people from head office in Bombay to local branches there, as the head office was over-staffed and people transferred to branches would not only get practical training in banking, but this would also improve efficiency in service. He was very upset at my approach. In the meantime, while I was away to London and after he joined the bank, he had closed down most of the training centres, which had taken me more than two years to establish. I never asked him the reason for his closing down the training centres. Even before these episodes took place, he would punctuate all the discussions with the executives by calling us 'barbers', which I thought meant that we were inexperienced clerks. He had many qualities like dedication, devotion and conviction.

An Officer on Special Duty, one P.K. Iyer, was deputed by RBI to Central Bank of India from 2 June 1970, a couple of months after the London fraud came to light. It was stated in his deputation letter that he would be reporting to the Custodian of the bank. He started asserting himself in all matters, making the staff feel that he ranked next to the Custodian. He took charge of the bank by issuing a circular that all papers to the Custodian should be routed through him. Not being accustomed to taking decisions, he nearly brought the working of the bank to a halt by not knowing what to do.

On my visit to India in early October 1971 for consultations, I found the situation not very conducive to the smooth working of the bank. Conversely, Iyer and Adarkar found that I was not likely to fall in line with their way of thinking and manner of working. On the morning of 13 November 1971, Adarkar phoned me at my residence in Bombay saying that the Board had permanently transferred me to London as Manager of the branch in the rank of Assistant General Manager and to look after the fraud case. (Between May 1970 to November 1971, I was on deputation to London from time to time only to look after the fraud case.) I expressed my thanks to him, came to the office, prepared the list of 13 departments which I was looking after, before proceeding to London a year-and-a-half earlier, and proposed the names of people to whom my duties could be transferred. Then I took the paper to Adarkar, which he approved immediately. I told him that I had vacated my office cabin and would be making preparations to leave for London at the earliest. I thanked him for all the courtesies and guidance that he had extended to me from time to time.

Working as Deputy General Manager of Central Bank of India, Bombay

After the conclusion of the cases in London, and on my return to India on 1 May 1973, I took over charge as Deputy General Manager of Central Bank of India. My duties covered the operational side of banking, including preparation and finalization of the balance sheet. After a few days, I found that 11,000 fresh employees over the base of 17,000 had been recruited in my absence with a view to create a massive infrastructure of chief officers, managers and senior managers, deputy zonal managers, divisional managers, zonal managers and a host of assistant general managers, a deputy general manager and a general manager. The internal audit department had been widely expanded. A new building was acquired for administrative head office, comprising 11 floors at a hefty rent. It was being fully furnished, even though Adarkar himself refused to shift there. (The Central Government was alarmed at these developments and appointed a Committee comprising retired Indian Bank Chairman, R.N. Chittoor and representatives of the Central Government and RBI. The committee submitted its report just when I left the bank). Earlier, A.H. Elias Committee had been appointed to oversee the work of the Chittoor Committee. Elias was a retired senior executive of State Bank of India. Earlier, Elias had a brief spell as an advisor to Central Bank. Meanwhile, Adarkar fell ill with an angina problem. Except for attending board meetings, Adarkar would only come to the bank when he was feeling a little better. The day-to-day management of the bank was left at the care of a committee comprising P.B. Tipnis, the General Manager, Krishna Iyer and myself.

Appointment as Chairman and Managing Director of Central Bank of India, Head Office, Bombay

On 1 April 1974, I was appointed Chairman and Managing Director of the bank for a year. On expiry of the term in April 1975, my services were not renewed. I was given to understand that RBI had proposed and the Finance Ministry had endorsed that I should be given an extension in my term another four years. The authorities appeared to have taken into account, among other things, that in the very first year of my tenure, the bank had shown the highest ever profit in its own history, considering the fact that the bank was operating on a token profit a year earlier. The reasons for my termination are explained subsequently in this chapter.

During my first year as Chairman and Managing Director, between 1 April 1974 to 30 April 1975, I organized four conferences of zonal managers.

Each conference had a unique approach. In one conference, representatives of the Department of Banking were invited; in another conference, representatives of RBI and the Board were invited; in another, representatives of the recognized union from all over the country were invited. The general secretary of the recognized union, who was also a Director on the Board, participated in three out of the four conferences. I wanted to make the management and day to day running of the bank, open, participative, transparent and efficient. I also wanted to give three other messages:

The customer service must be of the highest order and internal book-keeping must receive topmost priority. If these two issues were taken care of, deposit mobilization would automatically follow. Agents of branches and other senior controlling staff were required to concentrate on attaining high profitability. As the year of my term was nearing its end, a board meeting was held on 11 April 1975. Romesh Thapar and M.G. Balasubramaniam did not participate in the meeting. At this Board Meeting, apart from the senior executives at the head office, all the zonal managers were also present. The meeting turned out to be a complete shock and disillusionment to me. Representatives of three different groups of statutory auditors were present in the meeting. It was reported that there were many deficiencies in the functioning of the bank in so far as several branches had submitted inadequate and incomplete returns. There were entries outstanding in inter-branch reconciliation for a decade or more. Almost 10 per cent of the branches had not balanced their books for the year concluded. A large number of branches had not cared to submit to the head office many control returns and some branches had not submitted any returns at all! The total number of branches on that date was 1,220. Concurrent audit reports were even more damaging. Managers and accountants were reporting late at work and leaving early. Contractual overtime was being paid almost as a routine. During this Board Meeting, I was told by the auditors that the practice of contractual overtime was prevalent, in spite of their having received bonus and after given a solemn undertaking that they would not resort to their practice of contractual overtime. It was a coincidence that my term was not renewed, but I had a bitter lesson to learn that my management policies had not produced all the results that I had anticipated.

Romesh Thapar, Director, Central Bank of India

Before I settled down in my position as Chairman and Managing Director, I had taken Romesh Thapar into confidence, giving him a broad indication of the likely pressures that I might face. I told Thapar at a dinner in 1974 in New Delhi, where his wife, the eminent writer, Raj Thapar was also present that I depended on Thapar to ensure that I stuck to the correct and honest path.

I quote certain pertinent extracts from Raj Thapar's book *All These Years* (pp. 384–403).

> "Romesh had been asked to join by Dhar Sahib or Haksar, I can't remember who. He had protested mainly because

of his complete innocence about matters such as banking; they had wanted someone vigilant like him, so there he was...

"... The Chairman was due for retirement and the Board had constituted a small committee to go through work records and look for the next Chairman from within the organisation. After much interviewing, the name that emerged was that of Dharamvir Taneja, but before the committee could make the final selection, the government, that is the PM, had sent the same name up and Taneja was appointed for one year, which was the tenure...

Raj Thapar continues: "... Taneja had done very well with the Central Bank. As his first year drew to a close, the bank was out of the red, the rural schemes were under way, there was a considerable rapport between the executives, the communist director representing the workers had finally agreed to flush out those who had been obstrepous, like forcing managers to take off their trousers, and even Romesh with his scant knowledge of banking, no knowledge at all really, was caught up in the excitement of seeing plans reaching fruition." Raj Thapar further explains as follows: "Taneja's tenure had to be renewed and no one suspected any hitch considering that the Finance Ministry had given him an excellent chit. One morning Romesh received a telephone call from the Bombay office to say that Taneja had been dropped. He thought it was a mistake at first but then hurried to Dhar Sahib asking for an explanation. 'Apparently, Taneja has been colluding with the communists,' said Dhar Sahib.

Romesh nearly hit the ceiling then went through a long description of how they had disciplined the unions with the help of union leaders and the whole story from A to Z. Dhar Sahib was convinced and made desperate efforts for the next twenty-four hours to get the decision reversed. She would listen, seem to agree, disappear into an inner room, emerge from it tight-lipped and refused again. It was like a charade and very clear that Sanjay was not letting her off the hook.

Raj Thapar further elaborates: "Then something happened which must surely be unique in the history of such events. A delegation of senior executives of the bank, headed by Ratan Pochkhanawala who was the General Manager, came to Delhi with a petition for the Prime Minister, appealing to her to keep Taneja on. It had no effect.

"... Romesh, meanwhile, had asked for a board meeting. He was sworn to secrecy because of Taneja from whom we got the impression that his life would be in danger if the newspapers got hold of the story.

Raj Thapar continues her narrative: "Meanwhile, the Taneja affair worked on to its end. The Board meeting was called at Romesh's insistence but when he rang the Finance Minister, C. Subramaniam, asking for an urgent appointment to clarify some problems, the reply was, 'The Minister says he has no time in the foreseeable future.' No time to meet with a few directors of the leading government bank. It was outrageous, something Romesh had not expected particularly as he had known Subramaniam well. I have an entry for 18 May: 'It has been a traumatic two weeks. Romesh resigned from the

Board. All very sudden but he had to do it. The three other outside members had promised to leave with him but their courage failed them when the time came…"

THE RAJYA SABHA DEBATE

On 7 May 1975 there was a debate in Rajya Sabha, Upper House of Parliament about my removal from Central Bank initiated by Bhupesh Gupta (Communist Party of India) Extracts from his speech are given below:

> "…We have come to know that Mr. Taneja—I do not know who he is—has not been given extension due to some extraneous pressure, despite the fact that your Ministry, Department of Banking of your Ministry, and Reserve Bank has recommended, I am told, that Mr. Taneja, Chairman of the Board of Directors of the Central Bank, should be given extension. I have got some information, but I am not divulging it…
>
> "What is disputed is this that this appointment has been made or the extension had not been given in the case of the Chairman of the Board of Directors of the Central Bank in disregard of certain initial recommendations in favour of an extension. And I mentioned the Reserve Bank in this connection. He (Mr. Pranab Mukherjee) has not up to now denied that the Reserve Bank did not make any such recommendation. Well, we have also heard many other things and I need not to go into them. But somehow or the other, the whole thing has left a very bad taste in the mouth and it is being talked in the lobbies, in the press, and the Government should clarify the position by giving a more convincing answer.

"I am told that Mr. Taneja is not liked now because he is supposed to have good relations with the staff, that is to say, the employees. As you know very well, Sir, the employees are a very well-organised trade union here. And when I am making the statement, I do say with some sense of responsibility on the basis of the information that I have and which I cannot just dismiss. I have other information but today, I shall not bring that because it is of a very serious nature.

"... Why has Mr. Romesh Thapar resigned? He was a Director, a member of the Board of Directors of the Central Bank. Has he not issued a statement complaining of the manner in which the top post has been handled? And, Romesh Thapar is a man who is not a persona non grata with the Government. In fact, the Government appointed him as a member of the Board of Directors of the Central Bank of India and he finds it difficult to continue on that body because of the manner in which the top posts are being handled. Well, these matters certainly are open to suspicion and question. Now, I want to finish by saying, therefore, that Mr. Pranab Mukherjee should not encourage that habit because we know the Ministers also go. What is the guarantee Mr. Pranab Mukherjee—Badami has gone today—that tomorrow you will not go."

COMMISSION OF ENQUIRY ON MARUTI AFFAIRS

After the Janata Government came to power in 1977, a Commission was appointed by the government, popularly described as the Commission of Enquiry on Maruti Affairs.

Justice A.C. Gupta, who was on the Bench of the Supreme Court of India at the relevant time, was appointed as the Chairman of this Commission. The Report of this Commission is considered in a subsequent chapter.

An interesting aspect of this matter, which the Commission of Enquiry on Maruti Affairs could not have known at that time, came to surface when B.N. Tandon, Joint Secretary (Prime Minister's office) published a book in 2005, called *PMO DIARY-I "Prelude to the Emergency"*. The diary has the following notations about me on the following dates:

> 13 March 1975
>
> "... Devendra Sen (Director Central Bureau of Investigation) came to see me after the cabinet meeting. He told me two things. The PM had called him on Shivaratri day and asked him to collect information against Taneja, the chairman of the Central Bank of India. I was surprised because last year, acting against strong opposition from both the finance ministry and Prof. Dhar, she had appointed him as chairman. Prof. Dhar was unhappy. Later it turned out that the appointment had been made under pressure from the PM's house. Now it seems Taneja has incurred someone's wrath and the CBI's assistance is being sought to prepare a case against him. What a wonderful way to use government machinery!..."

Another entry appears on:

> 24 March 1975
>
> "... In the afternoon, VR (V. Ramachandran) showed

me a letter from an MP, Pratibha Singh, daughter of CPN Singh, to the PM. The letter contains complaints about Taneja, the Chairman of the Central Bank of India. Seshan (N.K. Seshan) said that he was certain that the letter had been instigated so that it could be used to remove him from his post. Devendra Sen has already told me that the PM has asked him to investigate Taneja."

There is yet another entry on:

17 April 1975

"... VR said today that the PM wants Taneja, who is the chairman of one of the nationalised banks (Central Bank of India), to be removed. Prof. Dhar is opposing this. Last year despite Prof. Dhar's strong opposition the PM insisted and ultimately appointed him to this post."

A further pertinent entry is on:

19 April 1975

"... I did not meet Prof. Dhar today but VR told me in the evening that the PM had talked to Prof. Dhar for about half an hour before going to the Vigyan Bhavan. For some time, the finance minister was also present at the meeting. They had discussed appointments to the banks. Completely disregarding Prof. Dhar's advice she ordered the removal of Taneja from the Central Bank..."

A criminal case was registered against me by the CBI in May 1975. A formal enquiry was instituted against me. In July 1976, I was informally advised by M.G. Balasubramaniam,

Additional Secretary—Banking Department, Government of India that the matter was closed.

The next chapter sets out in detail the conclusions reached by Justice Gupta, in his voluminous Report of the Commission of Enquiry on Maruti Affairs, dated 31 May 1979, concerning the termination of my services as Chairman and Managing Director of Central Bank of India.

18
Report of the Commission of Enquiry on Maruti Affairs

As discussed in the previous chapter, my deposition before the Commission of Enquiry was for me a very memorable experience. I could never have imagined that my removal as Chairman and Managing Director from the Central Bank of India would form a significant part of the investigation conducted by such an important and historically significant Commission of Enquiry. This Commission was appointed by a notification of the Central Government issued on 30 May 1977, just a few months after Mrs. Indira Gandhi had lost the elections. In 1977, there was a feeling of extraordinary relief since the infamous Emergency, which Mrs Gandhi had imposed on the country on 25 June 1975, was lifted.

I give below extracts from my deposition recorded by this Commission of Enquiry:

"During this period i.e. between April 1974 to September 1974, Mr. Sanjay Gandhi started putting pressure on me on four points (1) I must immediately sanction his Rs.1.5 crores loan for which proposal had been sent in December 1973; (2) that Mr. Wadia should be transferred as he was not responsive to his requirements; (3) that Mr. Kalra must be promoted immediately and (4) that some concessions be offered in rate of interest charged in different accounts. Regarding Mr. Wadia, I told him that he was a competent person. In any case he was a new person and must be given time to settle down. Regarding Mr. Kalra, the case was before the Selection Committee. Regarding interest I could not make any commitment.

"Mr. Kalra started behaving in a way that he was loyal to Mr. Gandhi and started reporting to him and everything which was happening in the bank. For example, Mr. H.S. Chawla, Mullahara Branch Manager, told me that copies of letters which were being exchanged between the Zonal Manager and the Head Office or various reports made by Inspectors and Auditors were being shown to Mr. Gandhi.

"During this period I discussed this matter with Mr. M.G. Balasubramaniam, Dr. R.K. Hazari, Mr. S. Jagannathan, Governor R.B.I., Mr. Ramesh Thapar, Director of the Bank and Mr. Tarakeshwar Chakraborty, another Director on the Board of the Bank. They all were apprehensive about the viability of the project.

"Arising out of discussions from the note Mr. D.S. Mulla was asked by us to visit Delhi to give specific recommendations about the pending proposal and also for his opinion if the Bank's existing dues were safely secured.

"I accordingly deputed Mr. D.S. Mulla who had experience of automobile engineering and was a consultant. His travel expenses and his fees were paid by the bank as Mr. Sanjay Gandhi was not prepared to pay for any consultant to look into this affairs. Two factors helped me to make up my mind on this basis of his report submitted to me in December 1974. One was that when the total project got completed to its full rated capacity, the total outlay was Rs.30 crores and 21 Lakhs at 1974 prices and the second consideration was that Mr. Mulla's recommendation of meeting immediate requirement of Rs.1.5 crores was qualified by his statement "that bank must ensure that repayment will be made within the reasonable period say 12 to 15 months." After I made up mind, I decided to call on Mr. Gandhi to personally convey to him about the rejection of his proposal.

"He further advised me that I should convey his decision directly to the P.M. or through her Principal Secretary Mr. P.N. Dhar. I debated the issue in my mind and came to the conclusion that proper Banking practice for me would to speak to Mr. Sanjay Gandhi directly as he was the bank's Customer.

"On 6 February 1975, I received a phone from Mr. N.C. Sen Gupta, Secretary, Banking Department, saying that he was speaking from the R.B.I Governor's cabin in Bombay and I should send him immediately a copy of Mr. D.S. Mulla's report.

"Mr. Sanjay Gandhi wrote a letter dated 01.08.1974 addressed to me in Bombay asking the Bank to confirm:

> "that the bank had carefully examined the entire finance scheme of the project and after careful consideration the Bank approved the finance scheme in principle."

"This certificate was required by Mr Gandhi to go to the Controller of Capital Issues for issue of additional capital. The certificate was not issued. It would have been contrary to the facts. However, Mr. Sanjay Gandhi continued to press the bank for the same.

"Manager of Advances Department, Mr. Kulkarni along with Mr. Shah were deputed to Delhi on 30.09.1974. They were accompanied by Mr. Kamath, Zonal Manager, Mr. Bhamgara, Chief Internal Auditor and others. They submitted an exhaustive report to me which highlighted the various deficiencies in routing and procedures which were still required to be completed by Maruti Ltd. And Maruti Heavy Vehicles Pvt. Ltd. As well as dealt with the status of the two accounts.

"On 24.01.1975 when I was in Delhi in connection with my mother's operation, Mr. K.L. Kalra told me that Mr. Sanjay Gandhi was very angry and wanted me to see him at once. I met him that night at PM's house. Mr. K.L. Kalra was present throughout. In a meeting lasting upto an hour or so, Mr. Sanjay Gandhi made the following points:

"That he had been misled into thinking that after Central Bank had opened a Branch in his premises, the bank would give him all the financial help. It was on that basis that he had agreed to the Branch being opened there.

"He was passing through great financial difficulties. He had ordered some machines and he could not get them as he had no finance to pay for them.

"If I could not give him money for Maruti Car Project, I should lend him Rs.25 Lakhs in the name of Maruti Consultancy Services Pvt. Ltd. Pending decision on this proposal which was at that time lying with Mullahera office for consideration, I should release him Rs.2 lakhs the next morning as he was in dire need of funds. I have now seen the proposal. It is dated 27.01.1975 and was for a loan of Rs.25 lakhs against machinery.

"If this was the way important clients were treated and commitments not honoured, proper people would have to be brought to head banking institutions. I thought this was direct reference to me as my one year term as Chairman and M.D. was expiring on 31.03.1975.

"Throughout the discussions he was rude, insulting, haughty and demanding. He at times became a little polite and cajoled for help. I got up when I found that Mr. Sanjay Gandhi was getting into fits of temper and could not control himself. Before leaving I told him that he had a way out of it, if he could get his car project approved in principle by IDBI. During the talk which he monopolized, he off and on told me in a commanding and threatening tone that I would not be spared. At one time when he was shouting one of the doors opened and the Prime Minister, Mrs. Indira Gandhi walked in and I got up to wish her but she immediately withdrew.

"I told Mr. Sanjay Gandhi on 08.09.1974, that if he would like to import technology for making a reliable car engine, I would be prepared to go to the Board and help him financially to import technology to make a road worthy car engine. He brushed aside my suggestion and also would not agree to any consultant to look into his project.

"A few days later somewhere in March 1975. Mr. Pahuja came to Bombay and with the assistance of Central Bank officers made a proposal to IDBI. I never saw that proposal (as I was on sick leave from 13.3. 1975 to 30.3.1975). I was informed that the proposal was declined by IDBI on the basis that it had no national priority. I had earlier met Mr. Chari, Chairman, IDBI to expedite disposal of the proposal.

Before leaving for Delhi Mr. J.K.Pahuja (G.M. Maruti Ltd) called on me, at my residence and told me that I had done a wise thing in rejecting the proposal. He disclosed that the engine which was fitted to the car and sent to Ahmednagar for testing had conked out on the way and had to be replaced by an imported engine.

"On 8 February 1975, Mr. Sanjay Gandhi spoke to me on telephone from Delhi. His was a monologue of complaints spoken in haughty and demanding language and threatened to deal with me properly. At that stage, I put the receiver down. On the same night Mr. K.L. Kalra conveyed to me the following message from Mr. Sanjay Gandhi which I noted down in my diary.

> "Unforseen, dire and unpredictable consequences would follow in not helping Maruti."

"While leaving for Bombay the same evening at the airport, Mr. K.L. Kalra and Mr. H.S. Chawla came to see me (23.4.75). They stated that if I agreed to see Mr. Sanjay Gandhi, it would be possible to arrange a meeting and a way could be found. Later, on 29 April 1975 when the Board Meeting was held at Delhi a similar suggestion was made by both of them. However, I told them that I would only see Mr. Sanjay Gandhi after the Government announcement terminating my term as Chairman and M.D. had been made.

"I called on Mr. Sanjay Gandhi on 1st May before emplaning for Bombay. He told me that he had me sacked for the following reasons:

"I had talked contemptuously about this car project to Mr. P.N. Haksar whom he described as his sworn enemy. I had also gone to Mr. Jagjiwan Ram who was wanting to replace his mother as P.M. with unfounded stories about his car. I told him that I had never discussed these matters with any of the people mentioned.

"It was a mistake on my part to have gone to Mr. C. Subramaniam, Finance Minister to convey my decision. This incensed him and his mother. I told him he was the Finance Minister and entitled to know of a decision which had important implications. He used vulgar and undignified language about Mr. C. Subramaniam. He stated Mr. Subramaniam was weak, could not make up his mind and was of no use to him and to his mother. He told me that he would be stripped off his portfolio soon and replaced by a person who would look after their interests.

"Central Bank and I as its representative had let him down and he would never forgive me for that. Besides, Mr. Kalra had shown him copies of letters sent by Central Bank Head Office objecting to some features of his dealings. He considered those letters derogatory and insulting to his position and lowered him in the eyes of subordinates of the Bank. He charged me that I deliberately got those letters written to humiliate him.

"He and his mother had been receiving scores of complaints against me. He was sending all of them to CBI for investigation. I asked him to mention a few. He said they were too numerous to remember. Mr. Kalra, However, had told me of the charges a day earlier. A few days later a case was registered against me. In July 1976, I was informed by

Mr. M.G. Balasubramaniam that C.B.I. had found nothing against me.

"He stated that I had put down the receiver when he was talking to me on phone over trunk line to Bombay. He had to ask Mr. Kalra to convey the remaining portion of his message I told him that I had duly received his message."

Extracts from the 'Report of the Commission of Enquiry on Maruti Affairs' dated 31 May 1979, appearing in pages 127 to 129, are reproduced below. Since this is a public document, these extracts are reproduced in their entirety. The extracts crystallize the stresses and strains that I had undergone during my tenure as Chairman and Managing Director of Central Bank of India.

> "... Shri D.V. Taneja was appointed Chairman of Central Bank of India but his term was not renewed after one year. The way he was chosen for the office and then got rid of gives an indication of the trend of things at the time. Shri Taneja was appointed Chairman with effect from April 1, 1974. In November/December 1971 he was associated with the deliberations over the Rs. 10 lacs interim loan proposal of Maruti Limited when he was posted at the Head Office of the Bank in Bombay. Before the proposal was put up to the Custodian of the Bank, Shri Sanjay Gandhi met Shri Taneja in Delhi when the latter came to Delhi sometime in October/November 1971. Thereafter in January 1974, Shri K.L. Kalra who was then Development Officer in Central Bank of India introduced Shri Taneja to Shri Kishan Lal Jalan and Shri J.K. Pahuja. On January 23, 1974 Shri Kalra arranged a meeting between Shri Taneja and Shri Sanjay Gandhi at

the Maruti factory. At this meeting Shri Gandhi told Taneja that "his machinery was lying idle and he wanted to utilize it" by manufacturing or assembling road-rollers in collaboration with Shri Jalan. Shri Gandhi also wanted to know when his proposal for a loan of Rs. 24 lacs to be disbursed in the name of Kishan Lal Jalan would be sanctioned. Taneja replied that he as Deputy General Manager had no sanctioning power. To that Shri Gandhi said that Shri Adarkar, Chairman of Central Bank of India, was due to retire shortly and that "search for a suitable person was on". On Taneja's next visit to Delhi on March 11, 1974 Kalra again took him to Sanjay Gandhi saying that Shri Gandhi wanted to "discuss his proposal for road-rollers" with him. At this meeting Shri Gandhi informed Shri Taneja that he had floated a new company called Maruti Heavy Vehicles Private Limited.

"Shri Adarkar's term as Chairman of Central Bank of India was due to expire on March 31, 1974. From some papers which this Commission received from the Prime Minister's Secretariat, it appears that on January 19, 1974 Shri P.N. Dhar, Secretary to Prime Minister, Indira Gandhi, recorded an internal note on the subject of a successor to Shri Adarkar as Chairman of Central Bank of India. The note runs as follows: "P.M. had mentioned to me the name of Shri Tanaje in connection with the Chairmanship of Central Bank of India. As P.M. knows the Central Bank is not in a good shape. Much will, therefore, depend on the new Chairman... The proposal is to appoint Shri Gutta of the Union Bank as the Chairman. Shri Gutta is a very able banker and enjoys a high reputation. Shri Taneja is at the moment No.3 in the Central Bank… As I have told P.M. I have checked on the relative merits and demerits of the two candidates from several sources including the Auditor-General, some officials and bankers. The proposal for Shri Gutta's appointment has already been made formally to the A.C.C. (Appointments Committee of the Cabinet) and is being submitted to P.M. by J.S.-1 separately. I would respectfully submit that this proposal may be accepted". Prime Minister Shrimati Indira Gandhi recorded the following observation on a slip of paper bearing the date March 14 (the year which is not mentioned should be obviously 1974): "I have expressed my firm views regarding this matter. I think Taneja should be given the post."

"It is a fact that during Shri Taneja's tenure as Chairman, he granted a number of facilities to Maruti Limited and Maruti Heavy Vehicles Private Limited. Shri Taneja had described before this Commission his experience in dealing with the Maruti concerns as Chairman of Central Bank of India. "The Maruti group of companies were not normal borrowers" according to him. The opening of a branch of the bank in the Maruti complex of buildings in Mullahera "was an invitation to pressures from a person who enjoyed wide Government patronage. It meant an announcement of the bank's mind that it was closely identifying itself with Maruti business". After a couple of meetings with Shri Sanjay Gandhi, Shri Taneja found that Shri Gandhi "was wanting everything to be done immediately and had no patience for rules, procedures and formalities." Shri Taneja states that Kalra who had developed a close friendship with Shri Sanjay Gandhi was exerting great pressure on him [Taneja] to "keep on releasing funds for Maruti Heavy Vehicles Private Limited". Taneja had known Kalra since the time he was posted in Delhi when Kalra also was working in the Delhi Office. During the period between April and September 1974, Shri Sanjay Gandhi started putting pressure on him regarding various matters, one of which was that Shri Taneja "must immediately sanction the Rs. 1.5 crores loan for which proposal had been sent in December 1973." Another point on which Shri Gandhi insisted was that Kalra must be promoted. Taneja states that "the more pressure Mr. Gandhi put regarding promotion of Mr. Kalra, the greater pressure Mr. Kalra would bring on me for Mr. Gandhi". Shri Taneja admits being "quite in a dilemma whether I could take the courage of transferring Mr. Kalra" but "felt that this would not be prudent at that stage." According to Shri Taneja from September 1974 till almost the end of the year, Shri Gandhi repeatedly telephoned him or sent messages to him through Kalra that "something immediately should be done to finance his car project." As the pressure from Sanjay Gandhi continued to mount, Taneja "could not bear it any longer" and he made up his mind "to take a decision one way or the other". He got the proposal for a loan of Rs. 1.5 crores examined by various people in all its aspects and their reaction convinced him that this was not a viable project. Taneja felt that "a stage had come when I must tell him that so far and no more".

Before conveying his decision to Shri Gandhi, Taneja saw the Finance Minister Shri C. Subramaniam on January 4, 1975 and explained Shri Gandhi's proposal to the Minister. He told the Minister that he had come to the conclusion that the proposal should be rejected. According to Taneja, Shri Subramaniam fully agreed with him and "also added that a snap election was round the corner. In any elections that would be held in that atmosphere, Maruti would turn out to be a millstone round the neck of the Congress Party." While Shri Subramaniam was being examined before the Commission, Shri Taneja's statement was put to him for his comments. Shri Subramaniam admitted having met Shri Taneja but said "I cannot recollect all those things he had stated." Shri Taneja himself conveyed his decision to Shri Sanjay Gandhi on January 5, 1975. Shri Gandhi "was very upset" and told Taneja that if Taneja put up the proposal to the Board, he "would have arrangements made to ensure that it would be passed." Finding Taneja hesitant, Sanjay Gandhi asked him to "think it over". When Shri Taneja was next in Delhi on January 24, 1975, Kalra conveyed to him that Shri Sanjay Gandhi was very angry and wanted Taneja to see him at once. Possibly this being a case of not a "normal borrower", Taneja went to see Sanjay Gandhi that night at the Prime Minister's house. Shri Gandhi, who was "rude, insulting, haughty, and demanding", said that "if this was the way important clients were treated and commitments not honoured, proper people would have to be brought to head banking institutions." "This was a direct reference to me," says

Taneja, "as my one year term as Chairman and Managing Director was expiring on March 31, 1975." On February 8, 1975 Shri Sanjay Gandhi spoke to him on telephone, it was "a monologue of complaints spoken in haughty and demanding language" ending with the threat that he would "deal with him (Taneja) properly". Taneja says that on the same day Kalra also conveyed to him a message from Sanjay Gandhi, which Taneja noted down in his diary; the message was, "unforeseen and dire consequences would follow for not helping Maruti".

Taneja's term was to expire on March 31, 1975. On March 22, a proposal was sent by the Secretary, Department of Banking, Ministry of Finance, recommending extension of the term of the Chairman of six nationalized banks including Central Bank of India. For Shri Taneja, the recommendation was for extension of his term for a period of four years. The recommendation was made in consultation with the Governor, Reserve Bank of India, with the approval of the Finance Minister Shri C. Subramaniam. On this proposal Shri P.N. Dhar, Secretary to the Prime Minister, recorded a note on March 31, 1975 that the file containing the Finance Ministry's proposals regarding the extension of the term of office of the six Chairman expiring that very day "was received only this morning". The note said "P.M. is unhappy that such important proposals should be submitted for approval at the very last moment." Prime Minister directed the term of the Chairman to be extended by one month for the time being. Thereafter Taneja's case was discussed between Finance Minister Shri C. Subramaniam and the Prime Minister. Shri

Subramaninam has described the substance of the discussion in his deposition: "She said there were certain complaints against Mr. Taneja which required inquiry and therefore his term may not be continued". While Shri Subramaniam was giving evidence he was asked whether it was not unfair to drop Shri Taneja merely on the basis of some complaints made to the Prime Minister without an inquiry. Shri Subramaniam's reply was "you should realize that she was the Prime Minister". It is not clear what this meant; she herself had told the Finance Minister that the allegations called for an inquiry and not that the allegations had been proved. Shri Gutta was appointed Chairman and Managing Director of Central Bank of India with effect from May 1, 1975.

"On April 25, 1975 the senior executives of Central Bank of India made a written representation urging "the Reserve Bank of India and the Government of India to consider the re-appointment of Shri D.V. Taneja as Chairman and Managing Director as we all feel that such re-appointment would be in the best interest of the institution". Shri R.C. Pochkhanawala, General Manager, was authorized to approach the "authorities and also, if possible, to place this representation personally before the Hon'ble Minister for Finance as well as before the Prime Minister with a view to conveying to them our unanimous feeling and as expressed through this representation." From the papers received from the Prime Minister's Secretariat, it appears that Shri N.K. Seshan, Private Secretary to the Prime Minister, recorded a note on a sheet of paper on April 26, 1975 which reads:

"Shri P.A. Narielwala sent Mr. R.S. Pochkhanawala, General Manager, Central Bank of India with the attached memorandum. The executives of the Central Bank of India wanted to see P.M., if it was possible. I told them that P.M. was very hard pressed for time and they could leave their memorandum with me and I shall place it before her. Apart from the points made in the memorandum, the only point he was making was that Taneja had been a Chairman only last year. He was a Deputy General Manager and was picked up by the Government to head the Central Bank of India. To drop him suddenly only after a year will have a demoralizing effect on the entire institution. He made it very clear that they were not questioning the right of the Government to appoint any body to the post of Chairman of a nationalized bank". Below this note Prime Minister Shrimati Indira Gandhi added in her own hand on the same day: "There were many doubts about Shri Taneja. F.M. himself was reluctant. I overruled him in order to give Shri Taneja a chance but reports about his activities are not good. His patronizing of a particular union had naturally brought him some support from the employees. But it does [not?] auger well. There is no point in my seeing Mr. Pochkhanawala. Also I have no time". She marked her note 'secret'. Thus she again overruled the Finance Minister and, on this occasion, the Reserve Bank of India as well. On April 29, 1975 at a meeting of the Bank's Board the Directors (Taneja was absent) decided to call on the Finance Minister to press for Taneja's continuance as Chairman and Managing Director. Shri

Balasubramanian, Additional Secretary, Ministry of Finance, after speaking to the Finance Minister informed Shri Taneja that the "Finance Minister could not meet the Directors in the foreseeable future".

"The inquiry against Shri Taneja was ultimately dropped for want of evidence. From the facts the conclusion seems inescapable that Prime Minister Shrimati Indira Gandhi opposed the renewal of Shri Taneja's term as Chairman of Central Bank of India overruling the recommendations of the Reserve Bank of India and the Finance Minister because Taneja did not find it possible to approve Sanjay Gandhi's proposal for a loan of Rs. 1.5 crores to help Maruti Limited."

For observers of Indian history, Indian politics and for the legal fraternity, I believe that the report of the Commission of Enquiry makes fascinating and instructive reading. It has meticulously documented instances portraying the misuse of power that had engulfed India at the relevant time. It is also a lesson for our future generations that never again must India ever suffer the ignominy of an Emergency.

19
Vignettes of Some Leading Bankers of Central Bank of India

This chapter is dedicated to the mentors that I had the privilege of working with during the period that covered the pre-nationalization and post-nationalization of Indian banks. I began working with the senior managers of Central Bank from 1961. My interaction with the Chairman, Vice Chairman and the General Manager of the Central Bank continued during 1964 till 1967 and thereafter post nationalization as well.

SOCIAL CONTROLS AND NATIONALIZATION OF BANKS

In December 1967, the Government of India introduced social controls over banks with a view to securing a better alignment of the banking system to the needs of economic policy.[1] Once social controls were issued, the Board of Directors of Central Bank was disbanded and the General Manager, V. C. Patel was given powers by the government to run the bank.

On 19 July 1969, 14 major Indian scheduled commercial banks with deposits of over Rs. 50 crore were 'nationalized to

---

[1] http://www.rbi.org.in/seripts/chro_1968.aspx.

serve better the needs of development of the economy in conformity with national policy objectives."[2] This was done pursuant to the fact that the Government of India issued an ordinance *Banking Companies (Acquisition and Transfer of Undertakings) Ordinance, 1969* and nationalized the 14 largest commercial banks with effect from the midnight of 19 July 1969. Within two weeks of the issuance of the ordinance, the Indian Parliament passed the *Banking Companies (Acquisition and Transfer of Undertaking) Bill,* and the latter received the approval of the President of India on 9 August 1969.

Supreme Court Judegement on Nationalisation of Banks: *Rustom Cavasjee Cooper vs. Union of India*

On 10 February 1970, the Supreme Court of India, in the case entitled *Rustom Cavasjee Cooper vs. Union of India,*[3] held the *Banking Companies (Acquisition and Transfer of Undertaking) Act, 1969* void mainly on the grounds that it was discriminatory against the 14 banks and that the compensation proposed to be paid by the government was not fair compensation. A fresh ordinance was issued on 14 February 1970, which was later replaced by the *Banking Companies (Acquisition and Transfer of Undertakings) Act, 1970* (Act No. 5 of 1970).[4]

Sir Homi Mody

Sir Homi Mody headed the largest private bank of his time, i.e., Central Bank of India Limited. I had the privilege of

[2] Supra.
[3] 1970 AIR 564, 1970 SCR (3) 530.
[4] http://www.rbi.org.in/scripts/chro_1968.aspx.

interacting with Sir Mody after 1956 when he visited the Bank. He was admitted as a Director on the board of the Central Bank of India in 1926. He served as a Director from 1926 until 1947. Between 1947 and 1952, he was the Governor of the State of Uttar Pradesh. Between 1957 to 1964, he often visited Delhi. I met him on each of these visits and continued to update him with reference to the bank's working in Delhi. Sir Homi Mody lent great respect and creditworthiness to the bank. In 1961, I went to Bombay for about six weeks and frequently coordinated with him with regard to the golden jubilee celebrations of the bank.

Sir Homi Mody very ably presided over the first Chief Agents' Conference in 1965 in Bombay during which he laid stress on better customer service and deposit mobilization. When social controls were enforced on banks, he left the bank in 1968. I remained in contact with him till 1968.

C.H. Bhabha

C.H. Bhabha was the Vice Chairman of Central Bank of India. He was appointed as the Minister of Commerce from 15 August 1947. When he vacated his office as the Minister, he was appointed the Vice Chairman of the Central Bank and he attended office until 1968. The bank executives used to consult him for guidance and advice. He was a treasure-trove of information on financial and commercial policies of the government. The bank greatly benefited from his close association with and understanding of markets.

N. K. Karanjia

N.K. Karanjia had the distinction of serving the bank for nearly four decades between the early 1920s until 1963. He rose from the ranks and had the longest tenure as general manager and managing director. He was very firm in his views and gave excellent direction to the bank. The bank made great progress during his tenure. He was responsible for my induction in Central Bank in 1956. I greatly benefited from his guidance and advice in interactions with him when he nominated me to assist in the Golden Jubilee Celebrations at Bombay in 1961 and whenever he visited Delhi.

P.C. Mewavala

An extremely genial and pleasant personality, P. C. Mewavala was the Deputy General Manager from 1966 to 1970. He served the bank in various capacities until his retirement.

V.C. Patel

V.C. Patel held the post of general manager from 1966 to 1970. After nationalization, Patel was the Custodian till June 1970 when he retired. During his tenure, he had to take many unpleasant decisions, including those that concerned the fraud that had occurred in the London branch of the bank. He oversaw the imposition of social controls and had the unenviable task of disbanding the Board of Directors as a consequence of the imposition of social controls.

F.C. Cooper

F.C. Cooper was a Chartered Accountant qualified from the United Kingdom. He served the bank as General Manager from 1963 to 1966 when he passed away in January 1966.

He brought about a sense of direction to the bank and was responsible for the First Chief Agents' Conference held in Bombay in 1965.

Ratan S. Pochkhanawala

Educated in London as a Barrister, Ratan Pochkhanawala was the son of the founder of the bank, Sohrab Pochkhanawala. He inherited his father's grace and wisdom and continued his great father's legacy from the 1970s to January 1978 when he sadly passed away at a rather young age of 57.

Noshir M. Mistry

Mistry has already been mentioned in the chapter pertaining to the fraud that took place in the London branch of Central Bank where he played a significant role in the investigation and was the star witness of the bank in the court case, which has already been covered in an earlier chapter.

D.N. Upalaker

A charming and affable gentleman, D.N. Upalaker served the bank loyally for decades and as Secretary to the Board of Directors during 1973 to 1979. He retired in 1983 when he was working as the Deputy General Manager. While Upalaker was in the bank and thereafter, he and I remained on friendly terms.

B.N. Puri

I had the privilege of working as an assistant to B.N. Puri from 1949 to 1964. During the period in the Punjab

National Bank (1949-1956), he was kind enough to teach me all about banking, guiding me at every turn of my career. He trained me about ethical banking and advised me not to be afraid while taking tough and unpleasant decisions if the situation so demanded. He also taught me the intricacies of practical banking and was a towering influence over me in my most formative years as a banker.

In August 1956, Puri shifted to the Central Bank as controller of the northern group of offices with headquarters at Delhi. In November 1956, I was appointed as a Senior Officer in the Central Bank at Delhi. I was attached to Puri's office to assist him, in which capacity I continued working until he retired whereafter I was transferred to Bombay.

Puri had a calm and calculated method of working and he gave a good demonstration of it while guiding the destiny of the Central Bank during his tenure of eight years until 31 July 1964, when on attaining the age of 60 he retired.

The Central Bank made fast and noticeable progress under his guidance in Northern India. Puri led an active and healthy retired life until 1984 when he passed away.

Each of the aforesaid personalities touched my life in more ways than one. I am fortunate in having the opportunity to work with some of the finest and most illuminating personalities in Indian banking history, who helped shape my banking career.

20
Nani Palkhivala: The TCS Story

In a telephonic discussion with me on or around 24 April 1975, Nani Palkhivala informed me that he had prepared my affidavit and booked flight tickets for both of us the next morning to Delhi with a view to get a stay from the High Court in Delhi against the non-renewal of my contract as Chairman and Managing Director of Central Bank. He could have either taken this initiative on his own or at the instance of some ex-directors or senior executives of the bank. I thanked him for his kind thought and the trouble he was putting himself through. It was overwhelming to see the care and interest he was taking in my predicament. I told him that I assumed this was the approach of a jurist. I then put a counter question to Palkhivala: what would be his advice in the matter as a friend? He replied that as a friend he would advise me to forget about it. He further stated that after my statutory leave was over, I should join the Tata Group of Companies as an Advisor. I thanked him for his advice and told him that I would abide by it. He further added that I would need clearance from the Central Government to take up the job as an Advisor with Tata Group of Companies. He added that whenever I had spare time, I should drop in at his office to collect the draft of the letter that I should send to the government about this offer from the Tata Group of Companies. I actually needed the Central Government's consent as during my tenure as Chairman of Central Bank, the Tatas had inter alia banking dealings with the Central Bank of India.

During the interval between 2 May 1975 and 1 January 1976 when I was to report for duty at Bombay House to Palkhivala, I was pleasantly surprised about the sympathetic interest which RBI took to ensure that some alternative arrangements should be made for my future career.

I was told by Dr R.K. Hazari, Deputy Governor, RBI that after clearance of the Government of Mauritius, I would be appointed to a senior post on deputation, perhaps as the Governor of their regulator, i.e., the Central Bank of Mauritius. I was informed that the RBI had sent the papers to New Delhi for concurrence, for which, in the atmosphere then prevailing, the necessary consent was obviously withheld.

As soon as I reached home after handing over charge to my successor, P.F. Gutta on 2 May 1975, I was visited by the Chairman and Directors of an engineering company who needed someone to steer that company out of the problems they were then facing. While we were still discussing issues, Dr. Hazari phoned me to say that they had proposed my name to the group as their nominee, to help straighten their affairs. Likewise, a group of friends who had known me for several decades, I.K. Ghai and P.L. Lamba of Kwality and Gaylord Enterprises, immediately informed me that they had appointed me to look after their organization. I did not accept the offer of the engineering group, but could not turn down the offer from my friends. I kept myself busy in the successive months by helping them, whenever they needed any assistance from me.

In the meantime, I wanted to take a chance to rejoin Central Bank in my old substantive post as Deputy General Manager. For this purpose, I availed the services of Gagrat & Co. Solicitors, in Bombay, who sought the professional advice of the former Chief Justice of India, Mr. Justice M. Hidayatullah. Justice Hidayatullah gave a written opinion as follows:

"The term appointment having come to an end, the Querist reverts to his original service with the Bank. In view of Section 12 of the Act, until his employment with the Central Bank of India is terminated (and this has not been done at all) he continues in its service. His working on the Board was a kind of deputation but it did not sever him from his service. Otherwise if he had been asked to take over as Managing Director for a month instead of thirteen months the same result would have followed, leading to a palpable absurdity. The querist continues in employment and would be entitled to rejoin and get remunerated. He cannot be considered to have retired because he had not." The Board of Directors of the Bank rejected my request at its meeting of 21 November 1975 as explained in Chapter 22.

•I reported for duty with the Tatas on 1 January 1976, and they appointed me as a retainer consultant. I was attached to Tata Chemicals Limited, which was then being managed by Darbari Seth as its Managing Director. He was a colourful personality. As soon as I would reach the office, he would ask me to sit with him in his room with a view to exchange ideas on diverse issues, including different aspects of the Indian economy.

In early 1976, after I had left Central Bank of India, Faqir Chand Kohli, Director-in-Charge of TCS, sent me a couple of messages suggesting me to meet him. He stated that I should be working with him instead of Tata Chemicals or Tata Oil Mills where, too, I used to spend some time.

As long as I used to sit in Bombay House, I would often see Palkhivala. Darbari Seth mentioned to me that I should write a book on my understanding, evaluation and practical experience in dealing with economic ground realities.

The volume *Economics of India* was written by me in Bombay House. At least half of this volume was completed in Bombay House, until I shifted on a full-time basis to TCS from 1 January 1977. I was given the designation of Consulting Advisor and asked to look after the management Consultancy Division of TCS. I was further to assist Kohli to establish contacts with other banks, as inter-branch reconciliation of accounts of all nationalized banks was in huge arrears.

I consider F.C. Kohli as the father of IT revolution in India. TCS ranks amongst the top software development houses in the world, apart from enjoying a formidable position and running highly successful software companies in India. It was a great privilege to work with this highly devoted, dedicated and committed gentleman, whose only aim in life was to make TCS one of the jewels of the Tata Group of Companies. Formally, he retired some years ago, but his towering personality still dominates the IT scenario in India. His successor, S. Ramdorai, carried forward the torch with great distinction. During my 6 year long association with TCS until 1982, my main occupation was to look after their management consultancy division. It was in the early 1980s that McKinsey & Company, the world's largest consultancy setup, arrived at the Indian scene. Until then, TCS used to be usually the first choice of business houses, particularly in the public sector, to turn to for guidance and advice.

I believe that there would have been no TCS if there were no F.C. Kohli.

In fact, it is important to describe my first recollections of my meeting with Kohli. Some time in 1968, I had gone to see Sir Homi Mody, at Bombay House where he had his office. He made a mention of TCS. Sir Homi Mody told me that one Mr. Cooper of TCS would call on me and give me a brief on TCS and would also let me know how they could help us. Cooper took me to Kohli in Nirmal Building at Nariman Point, Bombay where the TCS office was located. Kohli was overflowing in his enthusiasm when he took me round his offices. He showed me, in particular, the IBM 1492 machines; he explained to me how these functioned and what results they could produce to save time and energy of accounting managements.

My thoughts turned to the reconciliation of entries arising from business between branches of the bank. The concerned department—Inter-Branch Reconciliation Department—was in a mess. If the entries were not reconciled in the shortest time, there could be hidden frauds.

A circular was issued by me with my signature to all branches of the Central Bank of India that for effective management, a new procedure was being introduced. It was called *Qualitative Control*. To make the new procedure more effective, all branches were required thenceforth to send all correspondence connected with inter-branch entries in a separate cover marked: Central Bank, P.O. Box ... Bombay.

It was agreed between the bank and TCS that the latter would wield control over the incoming mail, who would open the closed covers and start processing the entries so as to match the maximum of them separately for each branch.

After the new system had been tested for a number of months and its reliability confirmed, the printouts were distributed among the concerned staff who all wanted the new system to continue to operate.

This was the first triumph of F.C. Kohli. He had laid the foundation of computerization in India.

After I left the bank and joined Tata Chemicals as an advisor, I met F.C. Kohli a number of times, who advised me to join TCS. I joined TCS on 1 April 1976, on a part-time basis. The arrangement was made full-time from 1 January, 1977 as indicated above.

When I was working in TCS, I wanted to understand and get to know Kohli. I told his ever smiling secretary that whenever F.C. Kohli was in the office and free, she should let me know. Kohli was highly pragmatic in his views; I used to feel relaxed listening to him in the quiet atmosphere of his office and profit from his views.

The decision to revert to banking and shift to Dubai, in 1982, has been dealt with elsewhere in this book. My decision pained Kohli and other Tata Group of Companies' Directors, who had given me shelter in the Tata Group when I was facing enormous problems from Mrs. Indira Gandhi, the then Prime Minister of India.

My professional code of conduct would not permit me to name the business units who sought expert advice from TCS management consultancy division. So far as I was concerned, I learned much more about the functioning of different disciplines in which business units, particularly public sector units, were engaged. One of our reports was mentioned in Parliament, and, as is characteristic of the government-managed units, the debate in Parliament was concluded by offering to put the TCS report in the library of Parliament. After working for a year on this project, simultaneously with other assignments, I made a presentation to all the authorities in the government in whose jurisdiction and involvement this particular business unit was reporting to. The hall in New Delhi where the presentation was made, was packed to capacity. After my team and I had summed up our recommendations based on data, charts and observations, the Secretary of the Ministry, who was presiding, got up and said, "If we implement the report we are damned, if we don't implement the report we are damned." That was the last I heard about that assignment.

Of course, consultancy reports, committees, and commissions have earned the bad reputation of working as a whitewash to shield the working of the government. One doesn't know whether any improvement has subsequently taken place. Nevertheless, it is clear that for many years nothing has been done to bring about any significant improvement in the aforementioned unit.

One can look upon such experiences from two angles: one that as a consultant we could not have done better, and, second the government or the public sector is so much embroiled in wheels within wheels of vested interests, with utter disregard to the convenience or service to the community and with the ever expanding bureaucracy, it looks like an expanding circle out of which there is no escape route. My association with TCS improved my understanding of the business world. I used to spend time with the Directors there as well as Palkhivala both on an official and on a social basis. This gave me an in-depth understanding of how the Tata Group of Companies functioned. If India had 10 similar groups as the Tata Group of Companies, observing the same transparency, ethics, mutual trust and confidence and ultimately give all their retained profits to charities, India would be a different world to live in. Until I was associated with them, Tata Sons was the Holding Group Company and held not more than 10 per cent of shareholding in most of the group companies that they managed. Only recently because of globalization, Tata Sons is reported to have increased their shareholding in all their major companies up to a point that no Tata company can be pirated, cornered or controlled by any other group nationally or internationally. The change in emphasis that has taken place in their working towards the use of the most modern technology in all their engineering and non-technology units is a tribute to the genius of Ratan Tata.

21
Eminent Personalities in Independent India

In this chapter, I consider some of the leaders of independent India and my impressions of them, since I had close interaction with them during the course of my banking career.

Pandit Gobind Ballabh Pant (1887-1961): CM, UP and Home Minister, GOI

Sometime in 1951, Lala Yodhraj and I travelled to Lucknow to improve the business prospects of PNB in Uttar Pradesh. Thakur Uday Bhan Singh, the Senior Manager of our Lucknow branch, was the best example of a person who could walk into the British Governor's residence without an appointment. He became equally comfortable with the Chief Ministers of Uttar Pradesh.

Both Lala Yodhraj and I had an appointment fixed for a meeting with Pandit Gobind Ballabh Pant, Chief Minister of the then United Provinces (now known as Uttar Pradesh). During the course of the meeting, Pandit Pant raised questions about the economic development of Uttar Pradesh. He mentioned the problem of the meeting, for extension of the irrigation facilities through canal system as Uttar Pradesh had the most fertile soil. In the discussion that ensued, the bank offered to finance the project provided the UP government was authorized to raise finance through government securities approved for the purpose of counting the investment along with the Central Government securities.

We also informed Pandit Pant that we were prepared to do more than meet their immediate needs, if the UP government's owned commercial establishments could be authorized to deal with us.

These terms were agreed upon. After a couple of months, I was deputed to proceed to Nainital to get the signatures of the chief minister, Pandit Pant, on the agreement between the PNB and the UP government.

On arrival at the terminal taxi stand at Nainital, I found a person holding two umbrellas. The rain was at its fury and we had to walk a couple of miles. The second umbrella, which was meant for me, was of no help as we climbed the hill to Pandit Pant's residence.

I was completely drenched by the time I reached Pandit Pant's residence. Pandit Pant had a remarkable memory for face recognition and name. He embraced me and called for his staff to get alternate clothes for me and to get my clothes ironed as they would not dry in the rainy weather. It was for the first time that I met Pandit Pant on a one-to-one basis. He was affectionate and greatly concerned that I might catch a cold. Pandit Pant was a victim of Parkinson's disease and I found that he was having great difficulty in putting his initials on each page of the agreement.

On his joining the Central Government, as India's Home Minister in January 1955, when I went to see him, he took me to his private study and asked me for all the news on economic issues. By this time, I was working as Economic Adviser of the PNB, apart from being the bank's Public Relations Officer, in which capacity I had gone to meet Pandit Pant. He insisted that we should meet whenever I wanted to tell him what happened in the economic and banking world. He was a fatherly figure and conveyed his views and feelings just by a slight shift in the nuances of his words.

I wish to narrate a brief and true story, which indicates the kindness and humanity of Pandit Pant when he was the Home Minister of India. This incident occurred sometime in 1957. I had some friends in Delhi at the time, whom I wish to describe by the abbreviation 'K'. They were two brothers running an import and export business. The elder brother had married an American wife while in the United States of America. The bride had joined the husband in Delhi, India and had given birth to a boy. There was a great rejoicing in the family but the daughter-in-law and the baby boy were finding their first summer in India suffocating. One night, the American bride disappeared. On inquiries, it was revealed that she, along with the baby, had taken a flight from Delhi, to Moscow to London and finally to New York, on a circuitous route so that she could not be traced or pursued. The grandmother was very fond of her baby grandson. When she woke up at midnight and did not find her daughter-in-law and the child asleep in their bed, she raised an alarm and started crying. The sons brought their weeping mother at

4.00 a.m. to our house. The two brothers kept on insisting that I take them to meet Pandit Gobind Ballabh Pant. I had never gone to the Home Minister for help. If I agreed to take the three-member delegation comprising the mother and two sons, it would be for the first time in my life.

The four of us reached Pandit Pant's residence at about 8.00 a.m. Hearing the sobs of the lady, Pandit Pant came out to see what had transpired. I briefly explained the problem to him, to which he replied that he would require a written complaint. A Home Ministry official would come and record it, which was done.

In the evening, at about 5.30 p.m., I was explained how the event concerning the lady went through after the Air India plane landed in London around about 11 a.m. local time. The London Police, of mixed cadres, armed with necessary powers from their foreign office, evicted the daughter-in-law and the baby son from the flight. A thorough search of the baggage and person was conducted but nothing objectionable like jewellery, according to the list provided by the mother-in-law, was found. Officers from the Indian High Commission tried to persuade the lady to break her journey for a day in London by which time her husband would join her in London and would persuade her to return to India; but she was adamant to continue her journey to New York, which she was allowed to do.

When a few weeks later, I called on Pandit Gobind Ballabh Pant and expressed my apologies for causing him disruption in his schedule of engagements and in his work, he said that he hoped that the episode helped me to cement my friendship with my friends.

Sir V.T. Krishnamachari: Deputy Chairman, Planning Commission

When Sir V.T. Krishnamachari arrived in Delhi to join the Planning Commission in 1950, I was asked by the Chairman of the PNB to visit him and show his personal staff the location of grocery stores selling South Indian products. He was a very kind and noble person and displayed an innocence about his views and ways. He asked me whether I could give him company every evening for a walk around India Gate.

He used to ask me questions about life in Pakistan from where we had come as refugees, particularly the irrigation system, the bulk of which was in Western Pakistan, and about the wheat crop on both sides of the Punjab and in Western Uttar Pradesh. He had been associated with the RBI as a member of the Finance Committee and he had worked as the Prime Minister of the erstwhile Princely State of Jaipur. When I gave him average deposit figures of Punjab as part of the Indian Union and also compared these with the figures of Gujarat, he was agreeably surprised about the prosperity of the Indian Punjab and the savings habits among the North Indians, particularly the Punjabis. This Punjab at that time included Haryana, Himachal Pradesh and Chandigarh. One day, he told me that he had been mulling over these figures but he could not understand how the deposits in banks were higher than currency in circulation. He had the makings more of an administrator than of being familiar with the workings of the financial world.

When I mentioned to him that currency got converted into multiple deposits through cash and credit system, he did not appear to be very convinced.

In my next meeting a week or so later, I had prepared a small note about the functioning of banks. I had this note typed and gave to him to read it at his leisure. I also gave him corresponding figures of currency in circulation and deposits of banks in the United States of America. Our future meetings became rarer, as perhaps he might have felt that I could have talked to somebody else and he would feel embarrassed that he was not knowledgeable on the basics of banking. He rose to be the Deputy Chairman of the Planning Commission. I met him again when he attended the Diamond Jubilee Celebrations of PNB on 13 April 1955.

Dr Shyama Prasad Mukherjee (1901-1953): Minister of Industry and Supply and Founder, Jan Sangh Party

After the General Elections in 1952, Lala Yodhraj suggested to me that it would be a good idea to invite Dr Shyama Prasad Mukherjee to speak at the literary circle of PNB. We had heard views of government dignitaries on economic matters and it was felt that we should also hear a prominent person from the opposition. Dr Shyama Prasad Mukherjee was earlier a member of the Central Government as Minister for Industry and Supply. Lala Yodhraj asked me to visit him and fix a date for him to come over to the bank to speak to our staff.

I called on Dr Mukherjee at Western Court where, as an MP, he was staying. The discussion of our first meeting centred on the conditions in the undivided Punjab. The main thrust of his question was that the refugees from Western Punjab—Hindus and Sikhs—adjusted to their professions or businesses with a lot of initiative on their part, but refugees from Eastern Pakistan were not feeling settled. I explained to him the genesis of the Arya Samaj movement and the contribution made by Swami Shradhanand and Mahatma Hansraj, father of Lala Yodhraj.

First, I emphasized the ethnic ancestry and climatic conditions of East India and West India. Later, I told him that simultaneously with the formation of the Indian National Congress, the Arya Samaj Movement and its constituents concentrated their thrust on social awakening through education. He told me that he had heard about the D.A.V. movement but that he never had had the time to study the social and educational implications of that movement. I met him subsequently, about twice or thrice, and we used to walk in the extensive verandah of Western Court at Janpath, New Delhi. He was a person of great intellectual grasp and asked me if my father could come and see him so that he could have a more authoritative and broader understanding of Arya Samaj. Unfortunately, he passed away before my father could meet him and our discussions remained inconclusive.

Aruna Asaf Ali (1909-1996): Freedom Fighter

Sir Homi Mody, in one of his visits to Delhi, asked me if I had ever met Aruna Asaf Ali. I told him that I had been reading about her in the press but had never met her personally. He mentioned to me that Aruna Asaf Ali had called on him and wanted her to be introduced to people who were representing the Central Bank of India in Delhi. He had mentioned to her two names—that of B.N. Puri and mine—and had told her that he would speak to us. I met her and she explained to me that they were looking for bankers for their enterprise, i.e., a magazine called *Link*, and they were starting a daily newspaper, *Patriot*. She also mentioned that the Dr Baliga Foundation had placed its funds at her disposal for social and political causes that were dear to her. I also learnt from her that a building called *Link House* was being constructed at Bahadurshah Zafar Marg, at that time called Mathura Road. In due course, banking relationships developed with United India Publication Limited, the company responsible for the publication of *Link* and *Patriot*. Later, we opened a branch of the bank in their premises. During the course of our meetings, she mentioned to me about her political relations with Prime Minister Jawaharlal Nehru. She also described to me that the *Patriot* was a mouthpiece for the Communist Party of India and the Soviet Union. Since the Central Bank was their banker, I questioned her about the source of their funds. She stated that apart from the Baliga Foundation and personal donations from other local well wishers of the Soviet Union, the publications were financed through business houses having commercial relations with the Soviet Union. Initially, I was shocked to know that the publications were getting some funds from sources friendly to a foreign power, but I did not want to embarrass her by putting forth more questions as she had laid all the cards on the table. Now and then she visited our house until we left Delhi for Bombay in 1964. However, she always offered to me any help I might ever need.

In 1967, among one of my visits to Delhi, Aruna Asaf Ali contacted me and told me that P.N. Haksar, then the Principal Secretary to the Prime Minister, wanted me to meet him. She fixed an appointment with Haksar so we could meet. She had indicated to me that Haksar wanted somebody in active banking to exchange views with him and she had suggested my name. The visit to Delhi was my stopover from Calcutta where large-scale agitations, disruption of work and *gheraos* were in full swing. I felt that a way out was to divert the attention of the people to constructive activities and provide an outlet for growing frustration. One idea that I developed was that Central Bank of India should allocate Rs. 20 crores and up to Rs. 20,000 was to be given as loan to build a house by those who stood in need of such help. This would provide shelter to the employed and needy people as well as those belonging to middle class without any shelter and in this way create employment opportunities for skilled and unskilled unemployed. It could be possible in course of time that people would get diverted to constructive activities, when other nationalized banks also offered similar facilities as Central Bank did, and more and more people were offered help.

LAL BAHADUR SHASTRI (1904-66):
PRIME MINISTER OF INDIA

After being sworn in as Prime Minister in May 1964, Lal Bahadur Shastri came to Bombay. Lala Yodhraj and I went together to attend the meeting of select citizens at Raj Bhavan in Bombay. While Lal Bahadur Shastri, after finishing his speech, was coming out of the hall, one of his assistants mentioned to him that I was the one who had to send a note on department of prices, which I should hand over to one Rao who was head of one of the intelligence agencies, but whom I had never met. Rao had already been spoken to and was awaiting my note. Some of the staff members of Pandit Nehru had been retained and it was one of the members whom I had earlier spoken to in Delhi who was reminded by Shastriji.

The theme of the note was that key items of food including wheat, rice, sugar, kerosene, animal feed and such other requirements of villages were controlled by traders/brokers/agents/*aarties* in *Mandies,* who artificially created shortages through hoarding, thus raising the prices. In addition, they acted as money lenders. My assessment while in PNB and later in Central Bank was that we knew their tricks of the trade as they were our main customers in undivided Punjab and later in East Punjab and Western UP. Prior to and after independence, they played a key role in the economic life of villages in India. They were also active in other food producing areas like Andhra Pradesh, Tamil Nadu, Maharashtra, etc. My suggestion was that a department of prices be created and all *mandies* should have Central Government nominees to keep an eye on the doings of the *mandi* traders and they should be kept under surveillance. With the help of an appropriate penal law to be enacted, some severe and exemplary punishments should be imposed, fear should be inculcated in their minds and they must be prevented from carrying out their nefarious activities.

In the present context, when one reviews the first 60 years after independence, the need for keeping these traders in *mandies* under observation and monitoring, with an appropriate prosecution department, still holds relevance. If such a department was created with powers of prosecution against wrongdoers, the backbone of shortages could have been overcome. Shastriji had heard about my views though I had never met him personally. The note was duly delivered to Rao for which I especially flew from Bombay to Delhi and spent a couple of hours with him explaining to him the broad outline of the scheme. Unfortunately, Shastriji died in January 1966 at Tashkent and I never pursued this matter further or heard any more about it.

P.N. Haksar Asks for Notes on Economic Matters

In my first meeting with Haksar around the year 1967, I elaborated on the Central Bank Calcutta Housing Scheme. In the meantime, he gave me a few subjects on which he asked me to send him my understanding of the complexities of the business and the banking world. As time passed, notes concerning subjects on which Haksar had asked me for elaboration and review were sent to him from time to time.

He also clarified that he was making this request in order that he could understand, for his benefit, and that of the Prime Minister Mrs. Indira Gandhi, to show to her that there were alternative approaches to different economic issues than what they were being fed by the structured economic departments of the Government. Practically all the senior bureaucrats and economic advisors had more of a textbook and theoretical approach. He also added that my initial inputs would determine whether my understanding and approach was worth its while to be pursued further.

After I had started interacting closely with Haksar, he told me that Mrs. Gandhi was impressed with the quality of my work. The Prime Minister wanted me to join her team on a full-time basis. He further assured me that the salary and benefits I was receiving from Central Bank would be protected.

I discussed this matter with the management of the Central Bank of India. I was informed that I could be relieved from the bank on the basis of deputation, so that I retained my lien on the permanent job with the bank. It would be a political appointment, and it could be terminated at a short notice if there was a change in the government or in the leadership of the Congress Party. I was advised by the management of the bank not to sever my relationship with Central Bank. Even though, ultimately, I never joined the team of Mrs. Gandhi, I continued to share my views on any questions that were raised to me and for which my written views were asked for by Haksar or by the Prime Minister herself.

After the last note of 15 March 1970, I was not contacted by Haksar to prepare any documents though I continued my social contacts with him until I left for London in the first week of May 1970.

On 30 April 1975, I called on P. N. Haksar at his residence at New Delhi and explained to him how my association with Central Bank had come to an end. He appeared to be disturbed and left me waiting in the room. After some time, he returned and gave me a letter addressed to the Prime Minister, resigning from the post of Deputy Chairman of the Planning Commission. He said, "Take it to the Prime Minister; this might help you." First, I thanked him for his gesture, which was characteristic of his nobility and of his consideration and association with me. I added, "Sir, this would complicate the situation further. I had decided to forget about the whole episode."

After joining TCS, I met Haksar in his office in Delhi and explained to him the work I was doing. Following P. N. Haksar's leaving the government, in consultation with F.C. Kohli, we invited Haksar to Bombay and he spoke to the TCS staff on the 'Makings of India'. In the afternoon, J.R.D. Tata hosted a lunch in his honour where all the Directors of Tata Sons, including Kohli, participated.

Haksar wrote to me a letter dated 14 November 1983, when I was in Dubai. As usual, his main interest was in the future of banking, for the nationalization of which he had worked very hard. In response I sent him a copy of a report where I was associated, detailing how serious the problem of banking in India was in its day to day management and this was thwarting the achievements of goals for which the banks were nationalised.

On my brief return to India in 1989, we started to spend some time together every now and then. Since I returned to Dubai again in 1990, I missed the privilege of meeting him thereafter. He had impressed me as an intellectual giant and a thinker during my 22 years' association with him and I learnt a great deal from him.

V.K. Krishna Menon (1896-1974): Former Defence Minister, GOI & Former High Commissioner of India in London

Sometime in 1969, on one of my visits to New Delhi from Bombay, a Senior Manager of the bank R. Srinivasan, told me that V.K. Krishna Menon wanted to see me. Both of us called on him at his residence at 19, Tees January Marg. I told Menon that it was a pleasure and privilege to be meeting such a distinguished son of the country who had contributed to the freedom struggle and played a key role in the service of the country. Krishna Menon mentioned that he often visited Bombay and he would like to be introduced to a person with whom he could spend some time. He stated that he was no longer involved in the political affairs of the country and was leading a retired life. On my subsequent visits to Delhi, he had gone abroad. It was only when I reached London that he touched base with me and started visiting us at our flat in London. I had made up my mind that as he had been involved in a few controversies, I would not touch upon any issue that might hurt his feelings. Later on, when we permanently shifted to London in 1971, I told my daughters that Menon longed for company, and that he looked forward to visit a family where he would be welcome and where could spend some quality time.

We used to have long discussions. I would often initiate the discussion largely or economic and social issues. I would like to briefly summarize the nature and different points of view on economic matters. I told him that since he was so close to Pandit Nehru, and was, for all purposes a member of his family who enjoyed his trust and had the Prime Minister's support, I could not understand why it was not considered important to give the Planning Commission a statutory character, so that the economic development of the country remained under direct control of the Centre. Practically all development projects had high overruns and misdirection and inefficiency, defunct technology, and corruption. He gave me a long history of how the idea of Planning Commission started being developed when Pandit Nehru was asked to prepare the blueprint of India's economic future. Later, the matter was examined by different eminent persons and committees who advocated the need for a Planning Commission. Our discussions shifted to famines and shortages of food grains for which both of us agreed that it was hoarding by merchants rather than actual shortage of food grains that always led to the crisis. It appeared to me that Krishna Menon did not know much about bazaar dealings in London in unofficial foreign exchange markets, until I showed him round a few exchange houses in London who used to display on blackboards the market exchange rates of Indian rupees against the pounds sterling and the US dollars. During one such interaction, I mentioned to him that so much time and energy of the nation as well as its attention was being spent on Non-Alignment. I held the view that the economic strength of India would alone earn respect for the country.

I may explain that the discussions on various points to which I have alluded here did not take place in a chorological order but were spread over a few evenings and occasions when he visited us or I had gone out with him in London.

In one of our outings in London, Krishna Menon took me to visit the Houses of Parliament in London where he introduced me to the Labour Party's Leader of the Opposition, Harold Wilson, and also to the Conservative Prime Minister, Edward Heath. These British leaders exchanged pleasantries with Krishna Menon and asked him for news about India at that time. Their meeting impressed me as it was clear that Menon enjoyed immense popularity during his erstwhile long tenure as High Commissioner of India in London.

On one point about the menace of parallel currency or black money, I had strong views and I gave Krishna Menon a broad outline of a scheme to deal with this menace. On his return to India, he explained the approach about demonetization to the Prime Minister.

On my return to India from London, Krishna Menon would call on us whenever he came to Bombay and I would do likewise whenever I went to New Delhi.

After assuming charge as Chairman and Managing Director on 1 April 1974, I met him a couple of times in Delhi in 1974, and, particularly, when Krishna Menon was in the hospital lying ill in a critical condition. Only a couple of weeks before his death, I spent about an hour with him in the hospital, where the doctor advised me not to strain him. He insisted on talking to me while he was wearing an oxygen mask; I could barely understand what exactly he wanted to convey to me.

Krishna Menon died at the age of 78, a bachelor, without any family member to mourn him. Many eminent persons including the Prime Minister were present at his cremation.

The affection and concern that Krishna Menon bestowed on us during a period of almost five years of his association with our family, will always remain etched in our hearts. As a family, we cherish the sweet yet sorrowful memories of this lonely and isolated, and yet a fine, kind-hearted gentleman and a loyal, patriotic son of India.

22
Interactions with Mrs Indira Gandhi

This chapter outlines my interaction with the Prime Minister of India, Mrs Indira Gandhi, at the relevant time during 1974. A great deal has been written about Mrs Gandhi and her *imprimatur* on India. My interaction with the Prime Minister was in the context of Indian banking and solutions to the country's economic problems that were prevalent at the time. The episode of my termination as Chairman of the Central Bank of India and the role of Mrs Gandhi in this termination have already been considered in earlier chapters, apart from the Report of the Commission of Enquiry on Maruti Affairs prepared by Justice A.C. Gupta. Nevertheless, this book would remain incomplete without a brief description of the meetings I had with her in 1974.

My first meeting with the Prime Minister Mrs Indira Gandhi took place on 27 May 1974, which was arranged by D.N. Ghosh, Joint Secretary, Banking Department, Ministry of Finance, Government of India, who told me that the meeting had been fixed at the instance of the Prime Minister. I had carried with me copies of a note containing different points, a copy of which I gave her. Mrs Gandhi initiated the discussion by mentioning that Krishna Menon was a family friend and had been speaking about my discussions with him. He had suggested to the Prime Minister that she might meet me to exchange views on economic matters. During the meeting, I stated that the economic frontiers of a nation required vigilance, measure of leadership and clarity of objectives. I added that the economic strength of a nation was the best guarantee against internal subversion and foreign aggression. I started giving one-line statements of my suggestions. Her observations and reactions to my suggestions are recorded below:

1. On my suggestion that in order to give priority to electrical power for use by industries and agriculture, government offices and public authorities should stagger their office timings making use of the morning's light and cool atmosphere, which would help to resolve partially shortage of electricity, the Prime Minister observed that staggering of office timings was not feasible.

2. The second point which came up for discussion was The Apprentices Act of 1961. I explained that the Act should be widened in its scope and should be made applicable to all banks and other commercial establishments in the country. Banks and other employers faced severe shortage of staff in summer months when there were vacations in schools and colleges, and parents in most cases proceeded on holidays either to their ancestral places or places of pilgrimage and tourist sites. Apprentices so absorbed, even on a temporary basis, appointed strictly on merit, based on their performance in the university, could have a lien to be absorbed in permanent vacancies in due course. Mrs Gandhi did not react to this suggestion.

3. The next point was the repetition of an exhaustive note I had sent to P.N. Haksar, her Principal Secretary, in 1970 stating that resources of banks should be primarily utilized for meeting requirements of established trade and industry and for building infrastructure like powerhouses, roads, railways and extension of irrigation, and production of essential raw materials. Funds should be also made available to good units in public and private sectors to make available medical facilities to their staff and the public. The banking system should help to improve the transport system in metropolitan centres so as to reduce reliance on the use of private cars. Subsidiaries of banks should look after agriculture and small-scale industries with an aim to reduce the overhead costs on the banking system. Her observation was that my old note had received consideration of the Government, but political compulsions and the RBI's thinking did not appear to fully support my views.

4. I mentioned to the Prime Minister that during my nearly three years' stay in London, it was customary for bankers to exchange views when they met at the Bankers' Club. I had also participated in a 3-day seminar organized by the Bank of England at Bristol University. My discussions led to foreign international banks making offers, purely on a commercial basis, mainly by western bankers, led by the United States of America, including France and Britain. They had paid frequent visits to India or had branches in India. They were prepared to provide financial assistance on selective basis in all infrastructure deficiencies whether in railways, roads, chemicals, fertilizers, power plants, etc. They were critical that India had no effective system of interaction

with counterparts in private sector banks in advanced countries. Further, it was stressed that this was the shortest route for transfer of technology.

The Prime Minister's view was that this approach ran contrary to India's policy of non-alignment, self-reliance and socialism.

(It is interesting that since 1991, India has liberalized its economy and is seeking Foreign Direct Investment (FDI) in key areas.)

5. I then shifted to the approach that India should concentrate on massive production of goods and massive exports, which were the shortest routes to stabilize prices and create employment opportunities. I cited some examples how the restrictive policy of the RBI, which the Finance Ministry supported, was in denying credit to priority sectors, involving infrastructure industries. In particular, I told her that machinery imported by the UP Electricity Board was lying uncleared, because the Finance Ministry felt that the funds must come from budgetary/plan resources of the UP Government. The Prime Minister made no observation on this point.

6. The next suggestion described below was not a part of the written agenda and the prime minister was already looking at her watch for the next appointment. I mentioned that I had taken a round of the villages of Delhi, and it occurred to me that various banks who had a large number of branches in Delhi at that time (Central Bank, for instance, had 50 branches and PNB about 60 to 70) could start adopting villages and concentrate on creating model villages with *pucca* roads, electric supply, and medical help. The banks

could provide extension of credit facilities, sponsor schools, build community halls and improve their communication with the outside world. Either she was in a hurry or that was a considered view, she told me that even though it was a very good suggestion, its implementation would lead to the opposition party, i.e., the Jan Sangh taking the credit for it. (This observation was consistent with the way she reacted, when in 1967 I had proposed that the Central Bank of India could consider extending housing loans in Calcutta to the extent of Rs. 20 crores for construction of 1,000 houses for the common man. She had then said that the Central Bank should not proceed with the proposal as the Communist Party of India Marxist (CPIM) would take the credit for it.)

Second Meeting with the Prime Minister

Initially, we were to meet on 9 August 1974 and I had reached Delhi on 8 August 1974, but as a consequence of telephone calls from R.K. Dhawan and N.K. Seshan, her Private Secretaries at the time, late in the evening on that day at the hotel, I was informed of the cancellation of the meeting.

The Prime Minister called me on 13 August 1974. I had sent her in advance three notes with a covering letter, which I proposed to take up for discussion. The fourth note on black money was already with her. This was the last and by far the longest meeting I had with her, which lasted far approximately two hours.

My presentation started with a reference to Note 1, which compared India with China. According to the American and British bankers who had visited India and China during the last three years (at the relevant time), India was well ahead of

China (1973) in terms of infrastructure (railways, roads, wool, synthetic fibre industry, and chemicals, pharmaceuticals) by at least 10 to 15 years not only in technology, but also in respect of the very size of infrastructure. Where India was lagging behind was in respect of our failure to evolve an effective system under which the basic requirements of our entire population could be met.

During that period Chairman Mao had apparently used the following strategy:

(a) He had tried to correct the imbalance occurring against agriculture, as industrialization gained momentum, by not allowing the bureaucratic elite to gain social status through various kinds of cultural revolutions.

(b) Second, whereas our industrial capacity, though 10 to 15 years ahead of China, was under-utilized to the extent of 40 per cent to 50 per cent, the less sophisticated potential of China was fully utilized.

(c) He used vast manpower by a combination of inspiration, indoctrination and political regimentation to put them to work and in return gave them shelter, food, medical aid and clothing, thus overcoming social and economic tensions.

Due to policies followed in India, there had been an imbalance between rural and urban areas, which created intra- and inter-tensions in both rural and urban sectors.

The other two notes dealing with constraints on credit were briefly touched upon. My view was that the country needed fast economic development, which meant that we had to produce more. Japan, when faced with a similar situation, had placed funds at the disposal of their commerce, trade and industry at 120 per cent of deposits with banks to accelerate production. My view was that the policy of the RBI was highly restrictive and was impeding large-scale production of goods.

Turning to the scheme of dealing with the menace of black money, I had dealt with the question on how the problem had arisen. The emergence of parallel currency owed its origin to the financial policies of the government, previous attempts dealing with it and elaborated on the mechanics of operations and the consequences. Most of the time during this second meeting was taken up by the discussion on the menace of black money. The scheme that I discussed is briefly summarized below.

The total currency in circulation in March 1973, as published in The Economic Times on 6 August 1974, was Rs. 9,231 crores. My note proposed that, say out of Rs. 10,000 crores of currency notes in circulation, Rs. 7,000 crores may be demonetized and replaced by new currency notes in much lesser amount. In this way any surviving 100-rupee notes from China or any other source would get out of circulation. The scheme envisaged that if the government succeeded in freezing currency in circulation, anywhere from Rs. 3,000 to Rs. 4,000 crores, it would have an effect as it would impact on the menace of black money or parallel currency. This would stabilize prices and improve in tax collection. All branches of banks, treasuries, post offices or places under government's direct or indirect control would receive the existing notes within three days. The new notes would be made available only in reduced volumes/amounts. The monies tendered in the form of prevalent notes would get frozen after deduction of tax in different slabs, where applicable, whereupon net amounts would be released subsequently say after five years. However, amounts surrendered would be up to a cut-off point, refunded to the public without asking any questions. Stated simply, all currency notes of Rs. 100 and above tendered would be frozen, would cease to be legal tender, and, only new notes at reduced extent would become legal tender as soon as the operation was over. The involvement of the armed forces, their communication channels and their assistance in transporting fresh currency notes to the same centres where old currency notes were tendered in circulation, would eliminate the chances of mishaps to a large extent. People would go to the same place where old notes were tendered. In exchange they would get new notes of the face value of Rs. 5,000 or less if the amount tendered was less. When I completed the presentation, the Prime Minister asked me if I had any reservation and if P.N. Dhar, at that time her Principal Secretary, could join us for further discussions. After he joined, both of us answered her questions about likely public reactions to the scheme and what repercussions it would have on the market. We were further asked to provide independent estimates of the cost of the operation. It so happened that we independently gave identical figures. This was the only time I met Dhar.

The discussion on this issue was the last time when I met Mrs Indira Gandhi on one-to-one basis. There was no further communication from her on this point.

Events in 1975 and 1976 and My Thoughts

I wondered at the time whether I would be one of the rare persons in the country in whose case the Prime Minister herself asked the Director of CBI (Devendra Sen) to see her on Shivaratri day in 1975 to personally investigate into my case and register an FIR in May 1975 against me. I was further told that when nothing was initially found, the Prime Minister asked Sen to find out something as she had been persuaded by her son Sanjay that the case against me was very strong and his sources were reliable and foolproof. (Apparently, Kalra, the Development Officer of the Central Bank, had taken a deputation of the local union leaders to convince Sanjay Gandhi that I was a Communist whose aim was to destroy their union.)

By July 1976, the case against me was dropped for want of evidence. The Prime Minister and Sanjay Gandhi were, however, successful in harassing me as their intention was to teach me a lesson for not helping the Maruti Car Project of Sanjay Gandhi, with a loan of Rs. 1.5 crores.

Justice A.C. Gupta of the Supreme Court of India, in his report dated 31 May 1979 of the Commission of Enquiry on Maruti Affairs, confirmed in his findings that the Prime Minister—Mrs Indira Gandhi—did not agree to renew my term in Central Bank as I refused to sanction Maruti a loan of Rs. 1.5 crore).

On 29.05.1975, I read in the Bombay Newspaper the following report circulated by U.N.I.:

"A high level enquiry into the circumstances under which services of Central Bank Chairman, D.V. Taneja, were terminated was demanded by Jan Sangh leader—Atal Bihari Vajpayee at a public meeting at Vaghdia in Baroda district today. Mr. Vajpayee charged the Prime Minister, Mrs. Indira Gandhi with sacking the Bank Chairman for not helping the Maruti Small Car Project with an advance for Rs. 3.5 crores. He challenged Mrs. Gandhi to contest his allegation and declared that he was prepared to face the consequences."

At that time, Mrs Gandhi was of the view that anyone opposing her son Sanjay Gandhi was opposing her. The person opposing her had to be eliminated and crushed. That is why she called Devendra Sen, Director, CBI to teach me a lesson.

The rest, as they say, is history. Undoubtedly, India will record the crucial role that Mrs Indira Gandhi and her son, Sanjay Gandhi, have played in our nation's history. I feel that the mood of the country in these years, i.e., from 1974 to 1975 was very turbulent, which ultimately culminated in Mrs Gandhi imposing the infamous Emergency on 25 June 1975. I became a victim of the twin wrath of Mrs Indira Gandhi and her son during these difficult years. It is my duty to narrate the true version of events as they transpired. Professionally, I have spent my life as a banker. We are trained to ensure that the hard earned money of depositors, which is entrusted to us, must never be exposed to any risk. As a trustee of depositors' funds, a banker must measure up to the highest yardstick of probity expected of a banker.

On 21.11.1975, the Bank informed me that since I had ceased to be in Bank's service on my ceasing to be the Chairman and M.D. of the Bank, there was no question of my rejoining duties on my substantive position which I held prior to my appointment as Chairman and M.D. I never resigned my job nor was I due for retirement. When I received the letter from the Bank, I was only 51 years old. My services were terminated without any justification.

23

The Middle East: Dubai and the United Arab Emirates

This chapter outlines nearly two decades of my professional life spent in the Middle East, from 1982 until 2001 and, more particularly, in Dubai, United Arab Emirates (UAE). These two decades have been very important for me, professionally and internationally as well. After my overseas experience in London, United Kingdom between 1970 and 1973, this was the longest period of time that I spent abroad and it helped me understand one of the most important regions in the world—the Middle East.

MAJID AL FUTTAIM, CHAIRMAN, AL FUTTAIM GROUP & MIDDLE EAST BANK LTD., DUBAI

In 1980, an agreement was signed between Tata Consultancy Services and Al Futtaim Group Dubai to form a joint venture to develop market-oriented software and introduce computerization in different enterprises in the Gulf. I met Majid on a visit to Dubai in June 1979. I did a sales talk with him that the Middle East Bank Limited, (MEB), which was a venture started by the Al Futtaim Group in 1975, in a Technical Management Agreement with Muslim Commercial Bank Ltd. (MCB) of Pakistan, be computerized through an online, live, all-embracing system. Under the Technical Management Agreement, the MCB was to depute workforce. MEB was wholly staffed by people seconded from MCB. Arising from the sales talk, Majid introduced me to the top management of MEB. In the ensuing months on a number of occasions we, as a team from TCS, paid visits to Dubai preparing the ground for computerization of MEB. A year after my first meeting with him in 1979, Majid was in Bombay during the holy month of Ramadan. On 25 July 1980, Majid visited our flat in Bombay and ended his fast as it was during Ramadan that he visited our home. He indicated that he would like me to be associated with his bank, MEB, and invited me to visit Dubai. As a result of our meeting in Dubai, he offered me a job and wanted me to join MEB Ltd. at the earliest. Since he had a joint partnership with TCS, after negotiations, it was decided that Majid could make use of my services on a part-time basis in the bank, while I continued to be employed and working in Bombay with TCS. Earlier, my resignation from TCS had been declined by J. R. D. Tata. This arrangement of spending my time both with the Tatas in Bombay and with MEB in Dubai continued for about year and a half, when I was given the option that if I was keen to revert to banking, I could be released by TCS.

MIDDLE EAST BANK LTD (MEB), DUBAI
(MAY 1982 TILL FEBRUARY 1989)

I joined MEB Dubai as an advisor in May 1982. This bank commenced its business in 1976. In 1982, MEB Ltd. was represented at the following centres:

1.	UAE	10 branches
2.	Hong Kong	wholly owned subsidiary of Middle East Bank Ltd. as a Hong Kong Finance Company
3.	Sri Lanka	1 branch at Colombo
4.	Pakistan	3 branches (Karachi, Lahore and Islamabad)
5.	Bahrain	An exchange centre
6.	Kenya-1	Joint venture
7.	Djibouiti-1	(Joint venture)
8.	Cairo	1 branch
9.	Sudan	1 branch
10.	Tunis	1 branch
11.	Nigeria	(Joint venture)
12.	London	1 branch
13.	New York	1 branch

I was initially conferred with the designation of Director Planning and Systems. From 1984 onwards, I became the Chief Operating Officer with the designation of Chief General Manager and Vice-Chairman Executive Committee and Secretary to the Board. My first assignment, when I got associated in 1980, was that the UAE branches should be computerized, which was accomplished by 1983.

In the initial stages, the bank had expanded at a very fast pace without adequate appreciation and understanding of the local conditions. A major area of responsibility that I had to shoulder was to recover non-performing assets. Over a period of time, and in some cases, in consortium with other banks, the MEB was brought to a stable footing. In particular, in Hong Kong, Sri Lanka, Pakistan, London, Zurich and New York, the Central Banking authorities and correspondent banks used to ask me to place before them our plan of action about the future of the bank. After an introduction and a brief comment on MEB's operations, the discussions I had with the Central Banking regulators (in the countries where MEB had its presence) would invariably turn to India as I was [and have always been], an Indian citizen. While the British and American Central Banking authorities were better informed about India, i.e., Bank of England and the Federal Reserve respectively, other centres and correspondent banks would ask me to elaborate on economic conditions in India. Perhaps, the Government of India would like to take credit for the impression that other Central Banking Authorities and correspondent banks at that time (1985-1988) had about India. They had great admiration for India. I used to put India in the best possible light that I could muster but it always made me wonder how people even in advanced countries, like Switzerland, had a romantic picture of India.

My professional contacts with the UAE Central Bank were from the very beginning, close and cordial. They showed great understanding and consideration (perhaps in comparison with other locally incorporated banks) how from year to year there was an element of progress, better control and adherence to international accounting standards in preparation of our annual accounts and the publication of the balance sheet.

My relations with the Chairman of Middle East Bank, Majid Al Futtaim, had been one of mutual understanding on the professional level. On 18 September 1988, I paid the usual visit to the UAE Central Bank. However, this time I was accompanied by N.H. Green, who had joined earlier as Group Managing Director of MEB. In the presentation I made to the UAE Central Bank authorities at Abu Dhabi, they made two points: one, they wanted the bank to be further capitalized, and, two, they made my continuation as operational head an important point of their support. I had already raised the basic issue of under capitalization with the chairman. As a solution, I had suggested to him that we should cut down on expenses by further retrenching surplus staff, but I did not recommend infusion of any further capital. In 1985, the bank had retrenched over 200 employees in the UAE out of the total strength of 500. Over the years, additional staff was recruited. At the time when I left the bank, the bank had expensive senior management. After I left the bank in 1989, MEB merged with the Emirates Bank International PJSC. Post merger, the merged entity did not absorb the staff that they thought were surplus, including the entire expensive senior management.

The balance sheet of the bank for the year 1988 was duly approved by the UAE Central Bank on 18 January 1989 when Green led the team of executives, including myself and the statutory auditors, Price WaterhouseCooper at Abu Dhabi. The balance sheet was adopted by the MEB Board of Directors on 7 February 1989. On 12 February 1989, the chairman, Majid, asked Green to obtain my resignation. I based my resignation on the fact that I would be shortly completing 65 years of age and wanted to be relieved.

Mirza Al Sayegh, Dubai Government's Director on the Board of MEB was also asked to put down his papers. My resignation was accepted the same day on the understanding that I would not part with any information concerning the bank to anyone. Thus ended my long association with banking as a career. In all the three institutions that I served, the end was abrupt, arising out of a crisis of confidence with the majority shareholder.

Transfer of Residence to India and Return to Dubai

I took a transfer of residence to Delhi in the first week of April 1989. I sold my flat in Bombay whereafter I called on Nani Palkhivala who conveyed his displeasure to me in no uncertain terms as to where I would stay. Palkhivala questioned me as to why I had sold my flat in Bombay without discussing with him as the Tatas wanted to use my services in Bombay.

However, N.A. Soonawala, then the finance director (and Vice-Chairman of Tata Sons) along with Ajit Kerkar, then Chairman and Managing Director of Taj Group of Hotels, asked me to take up the assignment of preparing a project report for either a mutual fund or a bank in the context of the situation then prevailing. For a couple of months, I assisted Soonawala and Kerkar while staying at the Taj Mahal Hotel in Bombay. In May 1990, I went to London with my daughter Ramni, an Advocate by profession, where Kerkar had already reached and thereafter we proceeded to Luxembourg to meet the Central Banking Authorities to get an in-principle approval for locating a financial institution in Luxembourg. In discussions with authorities in Luxembourg, Ramni's assistance and contribution was outstanding and her fluency in French very helpful. My view was that if the institution was located in Europe, where regulatory controls were transparent and clearly understood, the Tatas would enjoy a better reputation for whatever financial enterprise they established in due course. The project took about 4–6 months to complete by which time, Iraq invaded Kuwait. I received a letter from the Tatas that I should discontinue this assignment in view of the changed world situation.

On my return to Dubai on 7 August 1990, I called on Majid after a few weeks. He was gracious to offer me a partnership along with one of his nephews to organize a management consultancy operation. I probed the matter further, but did not feel convinced that there was any scope for such a business proposition.

I should at this stage clarify that Al Futtaim Group was a partnership between Majid Al Futtaim and Abdullah Al Futtaim, who were cousins; the sister of Majid was married to Abdullah. Both were equal partners in the main business enterprise functioning in the name of the Al Futtaim Group and at the same time were equal shareholders in the MEB together controlling a majority interest in MEB. Majid's eldest son, Ahmed Al Futtaim, and Omar Al Futtaim, the eldest son of Abdulla, had both joined the bank and I was expected to take charge of training them. Unfortunately, Ahmed Al Futtaim died in an accident but Omar continued to make progress and in due course occupied the position of Senior Manager of the main branch of MEB in Dubai in 1990.

In 1991, it became clear to Majid and Abdullah that MEB might not enjoy public confidence. The UAE Central Bank withheld permission to publish the accounts of the bank for the year 1990.

Before the bank was taken over by the Government of Dubai, who were obviously unhappy at the turn of events, Omar resigned from the bank. Omar and his father, Abdullah, wanted me to get involved with Omar Al Futtaim who started his own venture in the name of Al Futtaim Sons. I was formally associated with Omar Al Futtaim from 1991 to 1997.

If I were to look back at my entire career, I would consider those 10 years with Omar until the end of 2001, when I was still living in Dubai, as highly constructive and educative. In a matter of saying, I worked with the Al Futtaim family for nearly 20 years (1980-2001). My elder daughter Rashmi, who is highly qualified (MA London University and later MBA Edinburgh University) worked as a private tutor to the children of Majid (until 1985) and she also worked as a private tutor to the children of Abdulla from 1982 until 1997.

During this period from 1990 onwards, Dubai's economy was opening up and multinationals from the USA and UK were keen to establish their business operations in the Gulf countries. I assisted Omar in his various ventures. He ultimately succeeded in getting agencies of Hertz Car-Rental, Toys "R" Us, Marks and Spencer and Ryman. He also tried to get rights for Coca-Cola and McDonald's. The impeccable name of the Al Futtaims and the very high rating they enjoyed internationally as a business house, should be considered to be the one of the favourable reasons for Omar's success in obtaining agencies of these companies, which have spread themselves in other Gulf countries under the auspices of the Al Futtaims, except Saudi Arabia and Oman. Omar is a very conscientious and persevering gentleman.

While Omar was consolidating his businesses, with mutual understanding, the two partners in the Al Futtaim Group decided in 2001 that the business should not be run jointly, but under the control of one of the cousins. Abdullah gained the control of Al Futtaim Group. Now his son, Omar, manages both his own businesses and also the main Al Futtaim Group under the guidance and advice of his father, Abdulla Al Futtaim.

Association with His Highness Sheikh Maktoum Hasher Juma Al Maktoum

In February 1976, Tata Consultancy Services placed my services at the disposal of the Hinduja Group. I accompanied both Srichand Hinduja and Gopichand Hinduja to Dubai where they were looking at the possibility of acquiring a branch of an Iranian bank in local partnership with His Highness Sheikh Hasher Maktoum Bin Juma Al Maktoum. At that relevant time Sheikh Hasher was the Ambassador of UAE at Tehran where the Hindujas at that time were residing. After studying the pros and cons of the proposition, I strongly advised both Sheikh Hasher and the Hindujas not to venture into banking, as the UAE was being run entirely on the strength of expatriates.

My personal relations with His Highness Sheikh Hasher, as a friend, continued uninterruptedly to a great depth of mutual understanding and approach. He offered a number of times, the option for me to work with him but for one reason or the other, I could not accept his kind proposition.

However, in early 1995, when I called on him to wish him on the occasion of Ramadan, he took out a piece of paper and wrote down that I had agreed to join him and my orders would be deemed to be his orders. I persuaded him that such an approach would not work. However, I clarified that I could be associated as an advisor in which capacity I started working.

From 1 April 1997, I joined him on a full-time basis with a proviso that whenever Omar Al Futtaim needed me I could go and visit his office. This arrangement more or less continued when I left Dubai before the end of the year 2001. I was then over 77 years of age.

What I imbibed from my association with His Highness was more than friendship and understanding. He is a man of deep intellect and is sincerely concerned about the welfare of his staff. It goes to his great credit that those who joined him more than 35 years ago in his business enterprises, continue to be associated with him. I owe a debt of gratitude to him for giving me a better understanding of the true meaning of Islam as a religion—that it is a way of life of mutual trust and adjustment with compassion and mercy as its main pillars.

On four occasions (during the years 1998 till 2001), when in summer His Highness Sheikh Hasher travelled to Cannes in France, my wife and I travelled with him and his family, except on the last occasion when my wife, Kamal, was in India. His Highness is a noble person. He is a magnanimous individual, a gentleman of immense kindness and humility, and a great friend.

24
Reserve Bank of India

On 24 December 1990, while I was residing in Dubai, United Arab Emirates, I wrote a letter to Rajiv Gandhi, leader of the Congress Parliamentary Party. At that time, Rajiv Gandhi was extending support to the government of the then Prime Minister, Chandra Shekhar (10 November 1990 to 21 June 1991). As a consequence, on 30 December 1990, I was asked to contact the Governor of the Reserve Bank of India. In my letter to Rajiv Gandhi, I had given an overview of the then prevailing foreign exchange crisis. I also made some practical suggestions. The Governor-designate, R. Venkitaraman, and I discussed various options how to augment India's foreign exchange reserves, which had touched the lowest ever level in India's history.

On 31 December 1990, and a couple of weeks thereafter, I had an ongoing one-to-one meetings with the Governor who had by then taken charge. The core approach that I took in these meetings was that the sad circumstances in which India found itself at that time was a culmination of different economic policies followed by the Government ever since the country's independence.

What existed before the independence of India in the economic field was the result of entrepreneurship by Indians in the private sector, and, the policies followed by the British in their long association with India.

In the 43 years of independent India (1947-1991), at no time had the political party in power, i.e., the Congress, sat down with the captains of Indian business houses and organized labour, for a heart to heart talk of how we could build a new India with mutual understanding of each other's problems, accommodate each other and prepare the blue print of joint partnership. The Congress Party in power at the Centre gave slogans and the bureaucracy tried to give a concrete shape to those slogans by strangulating free enterprise.

The result was that the Government of India took comfort in slogans of self-reliance, a socialistic pattern of society, *Garibi Hatao,* and programmes and schemes for upliftment of the poor, which were never implemented in the proper spirit at that time.

A thousand corporate bodies were formed at the Centre and in the states under the auspices of the Central Government and State Governments (250 and 750 respectively), which aimed at ameliorating the lot of the poor and building infrastructure at various levels.

The private sector was asked to cooperate with the bureaucrats who were to execute the economic development of India through Licence-Permit-Quota Raj.

The private sector drew its own conclusions from the pronouncements and doings of the Congress Party and went about its own ways in trying to expand and enlarge the scope of their enterprises by such means as they could devise in an atmosphere of confrontation and mistrust.

During this period, the private sector accumulated enormous amounts of money through parallel books of accounts, evasion of atrocious taxation policies, created a parallel economy, financed politicians in power and in opposition through black money, and kept on transferring their surplus wealth to safe tax havens.

The labour force was badly treated by the employers, both in public and private sectors, who had continued to believe in master and servant approach in mutual relations. The employees retaliated against the management by raising impossible demands. The management and employees remained hostile to each other. The employers as the responsible party never took any initiative to win the confidence of the labour force.

Reverting to the economic situation prevailing in the country, the Governor was informed that, at that point in time, during my approximately 13 years' stay abroad in London and Dubai, I had acquainted myself with the trends and policies followed by international banks in the financial capitals of Hong Kong, Luxembourg, London, Frankfurt, New York and Zurich.

Further, I had largely dealt with the expatriate Indian business community abroad. In India, I dealt with practically all the leading business houses in my 31 years of association with the PNB (12 years) and Central Bank of India (19 years). In the emerging context, I would say that at the relevant time, many Indian businessmen perceived the policies of the government as anti-business, pro-labour and anti-free enterprise, resulting in mounting inflation and the Indian rupee fast losing its purchasing power. I further explained to the Governor that in my six years' experience with Tata Consultancy Services (TCS) (1976-1982) as head of their management consultancy division, I had been exposed professionally to the most lamentable and frustrating experience in dealing with the public sector enterprises of the government.

There was a way out by trying to stop smuggling of gold into India through *hawala* channels, which according to my assessment at that period of time, had exceeded 3,000 tonnes of gold accumulated in India since independence.

1. A simple solution was suggested to allow import of gold by NRIs so long as the duty of 15 per cent was paid in foreign exchange.

This suggestion was accepted by the Government while I was still assisting the Governor.

2. The second suggestion was to allow overseas Indians to acquire property in India so long as the consideration was paid in foreign exchange. The proposal that I gave originally was that HDFC Ltd. – Housing Development Finance Corporation Ltd., which H.T. Parekh, uncle of the present Deepak Parekh, Chairman and Managing Director, had founded, would acquire land, develop it, allocate built houses or sell developed vacant land, leaving it to the overseas Indians whether they wanted to construct their houses or leave it to HDFC Ltd.

The scheme was to be open-ended and start operating forthwith. The houses/plots could only be transferred to other overseas Indians. The idea was to build a foreign exchange reserve, which did not require to be repaid.

The proposal after discussion with other functionaries, including Deepak Parekh, and the Chairman, State Bank of India, was modified in favour of State Bank of India. Nothing emerged from this scheme. A modified scheme was announced under which the State Bank of India floated development bonds of 5 years maturity at the rate of 9.5 per cent per annum. The bonds were fully subscribed, but the rate of interest was high and the principal amount with interest had to be repaid in foreign exchange, thus nullifying the very idea of bringing in (non-returnable) foreign exchange.

3. Primarily, I had been told to help raise an indicated amount of foreign exchange from any of the financial markets that I was familiar with. Prolonged meetings and discussions were held. I wanted some letter of authority in my favour, which would enable me to discuss and finalise the transaction in the foreign financial markets. The wording of such a letter of authority remained unresolved and therefore nothing came out of it.

4. I had been convinced and I had witnessed it personally in Hong Kong, London, and Dubai how the exchange houses were freely converting Indian rupees into any foreign currency up to any extent. In Hong Kong and Dubai, and in other Gulf countries at that time, currency exchange houses were to be found everywhere. The flight of Indian currency had taken place not only through Hawala channels, but the Indian rupee was a physically traded instrument all over the world. I advocated out of my conviction and personal knowledge that the rupee was a freely convertible currency for all practical purposes.

Thus, I recommended, based on practical common sense, that the Indian rupee be allowed to float and in this way suggested that the government continued to buy foreign exchange against the sale of Indian rupees.

I recall that in January-February 1970, I had suggested in writing to the then Prime Minister, Mrs Indira Gandhi, through Haksar, (immediately after the nationalization of banks), that the supervision of banks, licensing of branches, credit control and priority, and sectoral lending should be taken away from the RBI. My discussions with various dignitaries at the RBI from the years 1990 to 1991 confirmed my aforesaid views. I did suggest to the RBI at the relevant time in 1990 to 1991 that there should be banking commissions in every state, representing different interests. These bodies should be statutorily independent of the government's day-to-day interference to ensure profitable independent banks and insulated from all types of pressures, which would result in practical and professional functioning of banks. The idea was to ensure that a banking commission would be giving directions in lending of funds in accordance with proper laid-down policies, conforming to the requirements of different states, under the overall control and supervision of the Central Banking Commission of India, operating statutorily as an independent entity along the same lines as the Election Commission of India.

25
Thoughts on Black Money

By avoiding the payment of taxes in India, and in violation of the laws of the country, those who have stashed their assets abroad in tax havens have earned the grand name and the title: 'Black Money – International'. So far as its intrinsic worth is concerned, the expression, 'black money', represents the wealth of the nation. The nation is entitled to make use of every single penny of the money that is illegally and surreptitiously kept abroad, for the development of India's own infrastructure. Those who have succeeded in keeping their assets abroad as also those who have developed assets in India on which taxes that are payable to the government have not been paid, are guilty of owning black money. The savings of national black money are easier to generate and convert into local assets and do not require international expertise or contacts. This black money has been converted into bullion, shares, real estate, investments in business and other speculative activities. That a section of the country's well-to-do business houses, who despite being involved in wrong practices since the 1940's have dared the government, speaks great volumes of their daring approach.

The subject has interested me and, therefore, in this chapter, I set forth my thoughts on black money, my understanding of it and my hunches about it. At the heart of the matter is the following rationale of the person who indulges in keeping black money: 'Who was taking all the risks that an enterprise entailed? We exercised all the efforts to make a success of it. When we calculated the profits, the government stepped in and said – you can retain a small percentage. Most of it belongs to us.' The businessman says in reply: 'Nothing doing. The government facilities are most inefficient and corrupt. Why should we part with most of our profits, which are the result of our hard work?'

I would like to convey my thoughts by dividing them into various historical sections. In Section I, I consider Gandhiji's command over India's directions of India's business interests.

1. The business groups had got together in financing India's war for independence from 1920's onwards, fully trusting Gandhiji's leadership for his integrity and trusting him so much to the extent that the funds entrusted to Gandhiji would not fall into the wrong hands. No one among the business community imagined that when India became free, the government of free India would promulgate the 1948 Industrial Policy Resolution, which in effect meant relegating the private sector into subordinate and meaningless roles. India was to have a planned economy and usher in periodic five-year economic plans as was the model and outline followed in the Soviet Union (Stalin, the dictator, executed the five-year plans in the Soviet Union by making the labour force work for these plans; if any section of labour dissented, they were sent to prison camps and millions of them were executed to make others obey Stalin's

commands). Was India's labour going to meet a similar fate by copying Soviet Union's planned economy? There was no individual freedom of any kind in the Soviet Union. It was one belief and one had to obey the Soviet Government and any dissent was forbidden.

After the Jallianwala Bagh massacre of 13 April 1919, and following that tragedy, the British imposed on India, the most ruthless regime. Thus the country had to fight for every grain of freedom and consolidate every gain under nationalist opinion and leadership. Under no circumstances was India going to lose an iota of that freedom. India was slowly marching towards its destiny to secure independence of the country where it was anticipated that the country would be guaranteed freedom of thought, speech, association and dissent. Its people would have the freedom to settle, seek any occupation, pursue any employment in any part of the country and engage themselves in all such business activities that would create wealth for the country.

2. In section II, I explain briefly the expectations of the private sector and how they would like to shape the future of India.

The private sector wanted to model India in line with the fundamentals of the United States of America. It was felt that America provided and secured all the benefits that were being sought for India. Only the economic might of America made it possible to turn the tide of war in the Allies' favour to finally win the Second World War. America had emerged as a leader of the world at a time when India attained independence. India was expected to seek the help of America to build its infrastructure and shattered economy.

Its currency, the US dollar, had at that time been accepted as a fully convertible currency in different parts of the world. The US dollars landed in India through the hands of tourists, foreign businessmen in search of enterprises in India and dollars being sent by millions of Indians settled abroad who sent remittances to look after their dependants and relatives. The bulk of incoming foreign currencies were fully convertible and were routed through official banking channels.

Before India opened its economy (1950-1990), dollars and other convertible currencies were available in India's import and export trade by a well-known method of under supply and over charge, resulting in leaving surplus foreign profits abroad, which were credited to the accounts of defaulting Indians in overseas tax havens.

After India liberalized its economy, it has been possible to build in two decades a respectable foreign exchange balance (mostly in US dollars) to give visible strength to the Indian economy.

Initially, the marriage between the incoming US dollars (which avoided being routed through official channels) and surplus Indian rupees (which emerged as a consequence of the functioning of a parallel economy) took place on an unorganized basis. However, once the volumes of the two currencies became large, some Indian entrepreneurs started parking their unaccounted US dollars in Switzerland and other tax havens around the world, and thus emerged the concept of black money bearing the title 'Black Money – International'.

The national black money was a very large scale affair. It represented the backdrop of the very large scale of operations of Indian rupees in India.

There were two types of Indian enterprises: one which had no books of accounts and the other which had duplicate or multiple books of accounts; one book showing little or no profit for the Income Tax department, the other for partners, showing some profit and the third, the real book for self showing the correct results. The dishonest operator was seeking an outlet for investing its surplus funds and has found an easy and profitable way by converting unaccounted cash into properties, shares, bullion and in speculation thus furthering the rise of inflation in India.

The country has caught the fever of rising inflation, which has also corroded the vitals of Indian economy and destroyed its healthy growth.

Indian enterprises continue to comprise the bulk of all types of business activities, which have no books of accounts but which represent the maximum generation of cash in all-round financial activities of the country.

3. In Section III, I describe how a section of the private sector reacted to India's foreign policies and India's internal taxation management.

For 40 long years until 2000, India followed the policy of non-alignment in foreign affairs but at the same time, heavily leaning on the Soviet Union. The Soviet Union ceased to exist from 26 December 1991, when the Commonwealth of Independent States came into existence. Many other East European nations, which broke their shackles from communism, gradually joined the European Union in 2004 and 2007.

Several sections of Indians during these years had no faith in India's foreign policies and looked with alarm with regard to India's almost sole dependence on Soviet Union/Russia for defence requirements. In 1962, at the time of Chinese aggression when the USA wanted to build for India a strong wall of defence capability, India spurned that offer because the Soviets told India to do so. At that time, America was a dependable ally whose views should have been heeded. India forgot that the USA had fed starving Indians with their PL 480 programme, supplying food for years until India became self-reliant through the Green Revolution.

Indians have been intellectually and culturally set to believe in free enterprise fostered by private capitalism and looked askance at various restrictive policies being pursued, reducing the role of private enterprise in India. Thus, for many decades after independence there were those who generated unaccounted rupees and stashed them in various free enterprise locations of the world.

This is the story of an era of surplus rupees in India, chasing unaccounted investments in India, which were kept secret as were the accounts overseas until the US dollar got transferred to the credit of accounts of several known and unknown Indians in tax havens. This is the saga of national black money and black money international, neither of which were respectable activities engaged by sections of Indian businesses.

As India advanced in its journey to attainment of freedom and beyond and events that engulfed it from time to time, there were reactions at various levels of its vast populace to the actions of whichever the government was in power. The cumulative effect of those reactions led to the emergence of certain policies that were going to shape the Indian economy among many other outlines that were the outcome of India's own thinking.

In liberated India, Indians were looking forward to the new government enunciating policies that would usher an era of a progressive system of government. They were hopeful of managing the maximum number of enterprises free from all government control, which would lead to a continuous spiral of growth and bring about a powerful and glorious India never seen before.

In free India, there were two contending parties: one, the power that ruled, and the other, the people that kept on understanding and evaluating how they were governed. Unfortunately, a section among them decided to put their well earned money not to any constructive use within the country but to manage their business in such a way that the resultant unaccounted profit would find a way to get credited to a numbered account in a foreign bank in free tax area. This story continues in its fulfillment even until today.

The one major factor that hit the economic system was the extent and level of various taxes, including the scale of income tax that would be levied. Those who produced wealth and from it, some margin of surplus cash in different forms must mainly and substantially share it with the government to prepare the ground to establish power houses, transmission towers/lines, steel plants to produce different types of machines to lay the foundations of rail, road and transport vehicles to move people, goods, vegetables and fruits from place to place in free India. There was unlimited scope for all-round improvement in the quality of life. However, for all these development efforts, the government of free India needed money to finance their operations. To a small extent the government could print notes/bonds, which the government euphemistically calls deficit financing, but the bulk of it had to come from income tax, wealth tax, gift tax, capital gains tax, corporate tax and import and excise duties. The government in various permutations and combinations has since independence levied all types of taxes on rich persons who produce wealth, but the totality of all taxes calculated together in their implication have often exceeded even 100 per cent of the money officially earned in the assessment year in question.

Currently, the levies of all types on compounding basis, when taken together, range from 50 to 60 per cent if truly and honestly paid in wide ranging activities of any large business house.

This imposition of different types of levies and taxes until the conclusion of the last century usually came to a total of 80 to 90 per cent, which the wealth creating class was not prepared to give away to an incompetent, inefficient, sleeping, directionless and corrupt system of government managed by untrained bureaucracy, and guided and supervised by the political class who only knew how to finance elections from Panchayat to Parliament of both houses and spend their spare time in making grandiose and irrelevant speeches.

The government on the one side and the wealth producing community on the other side have stood in conflict against each other, with the former trying to extract maximum amount in different forms of levies.

4. In Section IV, I wish to dwell on the importance of the Indian rupee, where it matters and where it occupies the prime place as the only currency that is the vehicle of circulation in India.

Ordinary residential colonies and high-rise buildings are so planned that shops to cater our day-to-day needs are constructed in clusters so that these outlets are within a walking distance reach of their residences. This is how small retail shops have established themselves in residential colonies all over India.

This type of facility is available in all small towns, metros and prosperous rural areas. These establishments do flourishing business but have no backup computerized professional account writers to place their final tally to have the yearly profits and loss accounts subjected to audit being made available to various government agencies. Sixty to seventy per cent of the nation's sales take place here and 90 per cent of items of mass consumption and facility of in-house services are available here. These are manned generally by self-employed persons and these persons sell items against cash where it is not insisted upon to give a receipt to cover the transaction. How do we estimate the gross amount available from 7-10 per cent margin that they may be making on their local restricted sales until we know every grocery, vegetable and fruit, meat and fish wholesale markets and at rates they mutually settle for supply and delivery of all items. In a rural-based economy with 30-50 per cent in villages and 20-30 per cent in urban areas of illiterate population respectively, as constituting backup forces, we should also note the entry of the other balance, i.e., the educated manpower who together move the wheels of economy on a daily basis. One can only admire the throng of enthusiastic people who gather together and manage and direct the large scale day-to-day affairs of these markets and their up and down effects on prices with 630,000 villages and nearly 200,000 other cities, towns and places of pilgrimage and historical sites and military cantonments coming into the picture. Their activities create a compounding and multiplying effect on the velocity of currency notes and coins including fake currency notes and coins that manage to enter our business system.

We have seen the tremendous flurry with which the great Republic of India bearing the burden of 1.25 billion souls goes ahead. These persons work untiringly on a day-to-day basis to run an economic, physical, social and cultural country; they are dedicated to maintaining and preserving their own religious beliefs to the pride of the country.

The totality of all these aforesaid actions performed diligently and honestly in close coordination every day for 365 days of the year without rest and without any mutual strife is a great tribute to the peace loving nature of all participants who manage the affairs of our multilingual country. All said and done, this clean and open operation has no clear bearing on black money. Perhaps some leakages take place in the direction of national black money and black money international. This has become an ugly feature of a section of those who conduct and manage our business affairs by rather dishonest methods.

The very powerful rupee is our national and proud currency that gives a day-to-day incentive to our internal accounting system, official budgets covering lakhs of crore of rupees where India raises huge amounts as income and spends it in managing its expenditure. The rest is met by deficit finance achieved by printing its currency notes for the required amount. Additionally, India waits in the hope that funds will flow into the country as Foreign Direct Investment, courtesy a rising faith of international companies and bodies corporate in India's liberal economic policies and the direction of our economic system. Nevertheless, the Indian rupee rules majestically, continuously expanding the business affairs of India through private enterprise. India today is identified by its currency symbol '₹'.

26

Postscript: The Silence of the Unknown

Bombay: Friday, 22 December 1978; Time: between 5.30 and 5.45 p.m.

At the crossing of Marine Drive and Babulnath Road, right opposite Lord Shiva's temple, while being driven home in the office car, I felt a shudder in my system. I tried to sit up and collect myself and found a certain vacuum around me. As I tried to concentrate on what that feeling could be about, a thought crossed my mind as a flash: 'Why are you trying to find Me in Lord Shiva's temple—I am inside you.' It gave me a jolt and left me completely blank. A few moments later, as the car drove on, I had an uneasy feeling that I had lost something.

On that day, the mind took to its wings; it was no longer a prisoner of my body. I could not feel its presence. It was not amenable to the body's commands—it had become independent. While the body carried out its commands without a pervasive consciousness, the mind, having an independent existence, was soaring high in the sky. It took a different view of the world. The mind has a personality of its own—a personality that I have continued to investigate until now. While inside my body, as its prisoner, the mind could earlier trouble me, agitate me, flutter and never keep quiet. It shifted from one subject to another, made me carry out its whims and fancies, participate in anger, hate, lies, falsehood and deceit. However, having bid adieu to my body, it had become free.

Another book authored by me (which has still to be published) will speak about the new friendship that has since emerged between me and my free mind.

The language that the mind understands and in which it only communicates, is truth, and feelings in which it extends and seals relationships, is love. However, this does not mean that the 'actions' of the mind are severed from judgements of wisdom. In the living world of facts and the strong interplay of powerful forces that are intent on mutual destruction, how can we save ourselves and escape their consequences apart from being caught in the paralysis of confusion. Hence, we need to wear the armour of love and truth. We must invite the voice of sanity. We must keep our cool and try to calm tempers in others so that a mutual exchange of views might be possible. We are living in a world of disposition where anger can give place to an unsettled mind.

What has been mentioned in the foregoing paragraphs would apply to a situation when a person who has catapulted himself to the central stage by circumstances beyond his control and his involvement and intervention could bring the situation under control and give such circumstances a respectable identity. In the normal scheme of things, where a person has achieved his goal of peace and silence of his mind, what else does he aim for or want? He will be living in the beauty of calm that he has struggled to achieve and enjoy that wonder of life. He would not want to get back into the warp of misery and again fight his way to sit on the pedestal from where he could achieve a control of his mind.

What are the facts of life? That all of us have taken birth and with love, care and concern were brought up to enter into a married life to give birth to a new soul. This cycle of perpetuating life continues until one's turn comes.

You anticipate that you may be told that you may retire from the all-embracing sufferings that are a part of your existence that you continue to face every day. Far from taking leave of this world, we need to ensure how we could avail the best of one's destiny, which would assure us the most beautiful future.

Our approach is that we have the most fortunate gift bestowed on us when we become a part of this evolution.

www.ingramcontent.com/pod-product-compliance
Ingram Content Group UK Ltd.
Pitfield, Milton Keynes, MK11 3LW, UK
UKHW041903230426